A LIFE WITHOUT

A Life Without Problems?

The achievements of a therapeutic community

Michael Little

with Siobhan Kelly

arena

Published by
Arena
Ashgate Publishing Limited
Gower House
Croft Road
Aldershot
Hants GU11 3HR
England

Ashgate Publishing Company
Old Post Road
Brookfield
Vermont 05036
USA

British Library Cataloguing in Publication Data

Little, Michael
    Life Without Problems?: Achievements of
    a Therapeutic Community
    I. Title
    362.732

Library of Congress Catalog Card Number: 95-76120

ISBN 1 85742 316 X (paperback)
ISBN 1 85742 317 8 (hardback)

All but two of the photographs in this book are from the Caldecott Community's picture archive and are reproduced with the kind permission of the trustees. The exceptions are those introducing Part One and the Epilogue, which show the Adam House at Ashford, Kent, the Community's present home.

Printed and bound in Great Britain at the University Press, Cambridge

Table of contents

List of figures in text

Graphs

Tables

Diagrams

Acknowledgments

This study has been rather unusual in its construction and there are, as a consequence, many people to thank. It has become customary with research of the scope undertaken at Caldecott to employ a research officer who collects and analyses the data and, hopefully, helps to write the project up. With such a large Community and so many areas of its life unresearched, we sought a different approach. We have employed several researchers to examine different parts of Caldecott and different aspects of its life and we have involved many members of the Dartington Research team in the process.

Those who have written drafts of the book have been acknowledged on the contents page. We were also helped by Hedy Cleaver, Pam Freeman, Stuart Harragan, Ken Hosie, Michael Kelly, Oliver Noakes, Lumsden Walker and Angela Williams who were all involved at some stage in the study. We have also been helped by Yvonne McCann, the unit administrator, and by Kevin Mount who prepared the summary papers associated with this publication and took or prepared the photographs used in the text. Special thanks go to Debbie Doyle who typed and corrected the manuscript at several stages.

We have been fortunate in the support of many outside the Unit who have commented on drafts of the book, proof-read the final versions or given helpful advice and support in other ways. Thanks go to Brenda Bullock, John Peyton, Michael Power and Pat Thomas.

The study could not have been completed without the goodwill and support of the staff, children and others connected with the Caldecott Community. It seems invidious to name individuals but several people have been exceptionally generous, including Christine Bradley, Jo and Peter Daish, Lucy Faithfull, Andrew Hardwick, Michael Jinks, James King, Simon Rodway and Margaret Stirling. We are deeply grateful to everybody at the Community for their time and patience.

None of this would have been possible without the financial support of two charitable trusts: the David and Frederick Barclay Foundation and the Nuffield Foundation.

Finally, our deep felt thanks go to the children, one of whom wrote a substantial part of this book and contributed greatly to our understanding of this area. For reasons of confidentiality, they cannot be named.

We are deeply grateful to them all.

Prologue

This is a book about the Caldecott Community, a residential home run on therapeutic lines for 80 children. It is a research investigation, covering the history of the establishment, the characteristics of the children, the interventions fashioned to meet their needs and the outcomes for leavers. It tests the effectiveness of Caldecott and similar places that help troubled children, but its construction is different from most scientific studies. Much of the book deals with the life of one child who lived at Caldecott while the research was underway. Many of the pages that follow have been written by Siobhan (pronounced Shivaughan) Kelly who describes the Caldecott Community from her perspective. It has become fashionable to talk about the 'child's view', indeed the need to listen to children is now enshrined in child-care legislation. Taking children seriously, however, and including them in research is difficult to achieve. We hope that, in some small way, by taking Siobhan Kelly seriously, we have added to the understanding of children.

By virtue of its construction, the book may be read in several ways. Some people taking a conventional approach, may read it from beginning to end. We have adopted a simple style of presentation and have used the minimum of specialist language, so we hope it is an easy read. Even so, it should also be possible to pick up the main messages of the research just by reading those sections written by or concerning Siobhan. These sections are indicated by quotation marks ["] and should add up to a story in themselves. More orthodox academics may prefer to stick with the other sections, skipping the qualitative evidence and concentrating on the facts and figures. However the book is read, the same conclusions should emerge.

In constructing the book, we have slightly adapted the data for the sake of clarity. We have brought together the children followed up in the eight living units that make up the Caldecott Community and placed them all in Woodside, where Siobhan lived. So Tony Bozzi who left in rather unsatisfactory circumstances was actually resident in Oaklea not Woodside and Siobhan never knew Billy and Brian Adams who lived in Lake View while they were at Caldecott. For the sake of confidentiality, we have also had to adapt some comments made by Siobhan. As the names of everybody directly concerned with the story have been changed, we hope this rather unusual treatment of research material will be accepted.

We are sure that the changes make no difference to the conclusions drawn at the end of the study. Had we produced a thunderously heavy-going *magnum opus*, the main themes emerging from the research would be exactly the same. By adopting the strategy we have, the results of the research should be more accessible and may encourage others to think of ways of presenting evidence on the child's perspective which adds to our understanding of services for troubled and troublesome children.

Part One

Introduction

,,

Myself

Full name	Siobhan Emma Kelly
Date of birth	18.4.78
DOA	27.7.90
Eyes	Blue
Hair	Blonde
Height	5 ft.
Weight	8½ stone
Family	Four brothers, mum and dad split up
Music	I like lots of different music including New Kids, m c hammer, rap and house music
Food	Frosties, chips, eclairs, chocolate
Place	Bromley
Friends	Katrina and Belinda
Books	Judy Blume, joke books
TV prog.	Neighbours, Eastenders, Birds of a Feather
Sport	Swimming, running, trampolines
Hobbies	Trampolining, swimming, running, athletics

"

My family

Dad: My dad is about 42. He is English. He sexually abused me when I was small and I will never forgive him for it. He is a lorry driver and works abroad sometimes. I haven't seen him since I was about four years old, and I would never like to see him again.

Mum: My mum is aged 38. She is Irish. She looked after me reasonably well, although I feel as if she didn't protect me. We argue a lot, usually over small things. She is alright sometimes though.

Brother: My eldest brother Kurt is 19. He also sexually abused me when I was small and has been in lock ups and a prison. He gets into a lot of trouble with the police, but I don't see him anymore.

Brother: The second eldest of the family is Barry, aged 17. He is very quiet. He is a bit of a hippie and is into heavy metal. He lives in a house with other teenagers his age. On the whole he is quite a nice boy, except that he's got a violent streak in him.

Brother: The next brother down is Adrian, aged 15 nearly 16. He is into hip hop and house music. He always has the top fashion clothes. He lives in a sort of foster home in Sevenoaks, he seems very happy there and is going to go to college to study social work and to do catering. I get on well with him. He's alright I suppose.

Brother: The youngest brother Nigel is aged 14. He is a pain sometimes, but I get on best with him out of all the family. He spends some time at home but he lives in a place similar to Caldecott but smaller, in Deal. I miss him a lot and would like to see more of him. We phone each other regularly.

,,

Siobhan's family tree

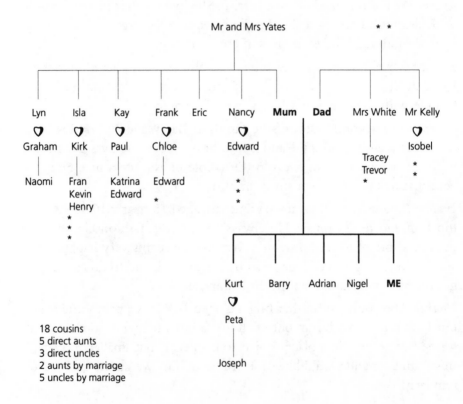

Mr and Mrs Yates   * *

Lyn   Isla   Kay   Frank   Eric   Nancy   **Mum**   **Dad**   Mrs White   Mr Kelly

Graham   Kirk   Paul   Chloe   Edward   Isobel

                                                              Tracey
                                                              Trevor
                                                                *
Naomi   Fran   Katrina   Edward   *
        Kevin Edward   *
        Henry   *   *
          *
          *
          *

                              Kurt   Barry   Adrian   Nigel   **ME**

                              Peta

18 cousins
5 direct aunts
3 direct uncles   Joseph
2 aunts by marriage
5 uncles by marriage

The hearts are Siobhan's way of showing marriages;
the asterisks indicate children whose names she does not know.

A Life Without Problems?

Introduction

The words which opened this study came from Siobhan Kelly, an articulate, intelligent 12 year old who joined the Caldecott Community in 1990. We have been quoting verbatim from her diary; the only change has been to replace her lower case 'i' with a capital. Siobhan, her fellow residents and the Caldecott Community are the focus of this report. In the following pages we shall explore their backgrounds, their circumstances and their prospects.

Siobhan kept a diary for our benefit for nearly four years. She begins by telling us that she had been sexually abused by her father. This entry, made a month after coming to Caldecott, is the first time that Siobhan freely admits to somebody else the nature of her maltreatment. As the diary was not passed on for 12 months, it was some time before either the residential workers or the researchers would know the source of Siobhan's misbehaviour and unhappiness. Unfortunately, neither we (the researchers) nor they (the residential workers) would have been surprised by the revelation.

The Caldecott Community has sheltered troubled children for more than 80 years. Not all have been sexually abused; not all have been as articulate as Siobhan but nearly all have required the nurture and support that such a setting can provide. But despite its long history, few people really understand the contribution of therapeutic communities such as Caldecott and, despite the frequent references to sexual abuse in the media, few really understand the needs of somebody like Siobhan. Hopefully, we can shed some light upon the workings of the residential centre and the wants of those within it. We are certainly convinced that it is impossible to comprehend one without knowing the other.

Understanding troubled children and thinking about ways of helping them have been fundamental to the work of Caldecott. Established by Leila Rendel in 1911, the Community has been part of a forward looking movement seeking new ways to help children. Indeed, research and development have become intrinsic to the Caldecott approach and this study is testimony to their commitment to this end. After all, few other centres would have commissioned a major scrutiny of their work at a time when the prospects for residential care were inauspicious.

What questions have we asked of Caldecott's work and how have we answered them? Initially, it seemed important to provide a history of the Community, beginning with Leila Rendel's pioneering efforts to aid very vulnerable children in the first decade of this century. We have traced the development of the Caldecott approach from the chaotic, warm and principled efforts of the founding mothers, through a group work ethos in the sixties and seventies to a broadly psycho-therapeutic model in recent years. Many records, letters and files have been dusted down, not least the case notes on the several hundred children who have slept in Community beds since they were first provided in 1911.

Naturally, the characteristics and circumstances of the most recent entrants are of most interest to those who work at or send children to Caldecott today. We have, therefore, looked more closely at all the children and young people who left the Community at some point between January 1st 1986 and the 31st December 1990. These dates allowed us to undertake a reasonable follow-up. Not all are like Siobhan, and several trends have been identified in the background, adaptation to residential care and prospects of the 60 young people who left during this four year period.

An ever present question in the minds of those who purchase places at specialist residential settings, not easily answered by those who provide the service, is 'What are the long-term outcomes for the children?'. We have, therefore, followed-up the 60 leavers between 1986 and 1990 to see where they live, how they get on with their family and friends, whether or not they continue in education or gain a job, suffer ill-health, get into trouble or remain dependent on the support of state agencies. As we shall see, while all children benefit in some way from Caldecott's ministering, we have been able to identify several ways in which the Community's intervention could be better tuned to the particular needs of different groups.

While the trends emerging from our historical scrutiny and the broad picture on the 60 leavers were essential for any assessment of the value of Caldecott's contribution to child welfare, more needed to be done. Although it looks after nearly 80 residents, Caldecott would describe its work as focusing on the individual child. Any conversation with staff about national patterns of child welfare usually shifts to the child they have been tending that day. We quickly noted that in Caldecott such conversations took differing forms depending upon the context in which they took place; the concerns of those coping with the older adolescents in Lacton Hall were certainly different from those working with the highly disturbed younger children across the way at Lacton House.

For this reason, members of the research team introduced themselves to each of the eight living units within the Community. They worked particularly closely with the first child to enter each unit during 1990. We came to know Siobhan in this way. As some of these entrants came with brothers or sisters, 12 children have been followed-up intensively. Our approach with these youngsters has been varied. Initially, we tried to get to know members of staff in the living units and asked them to keep us abreast of developments in their part of the Community. Like Siobhan, six of the children kept diaries or provided other types of written material about their life at Caldecott. We interviewed, at regular intervals, most of the children, although some were too timid, too disturbed or too young to take part and our scrutiny of them has been more distant. We video-taped some of our interviews and we also gave the participating children the video recorder so that they could interview some of their friends. All kinds of information, some of it very sensitive, was gathered and, after careful analysis, all finds a place in this report.

Even with this depth material, there were still gaps in our knowledge. Most important was to understand the perspectives of staff. In addition to our work in the living units we ventured into other parts of the Community; the school, the administrative offices, the kitchens, workshops, farm and stables. We also asked all staff, whatever their role, to complete a questionnaire about the reasons they joined the Community and their aspirations for the future. Some went further and described their working week and identified the joys and stresses of the job.

Everything mentioned so far has been about life within the Community. But, as Siobhan's introduction clearly demonstrates, fathers, mothers, brothers, sisters and other relatives, however abusive, remain a part of the lives of residents. So we have talked at length with family members. We also spent considerable time with social workers and other professionals providing support in the child's home area.

Finally, we explored the referrals to Caldecott in 1990, found out which children they accepted and whom they turned away. By following-up children who were offered a place but, for a variety of reasons, went elsewhere, we have been able to gauge the particular contribution of Caldecott to long-term outcomes.

Each part of the investigation has been conducted according to the rigorous rules of scientific research and the particular approach of the Dartington Unit which is described in detail in our other studies. But in presenting this material we have attempted a more unorthodox approach. We have juxtaposed and tried to link the various parts of the study with material on Siobhan's life before, during and after her stay at Caldecott. Her dialogue helps carry the book forward. We hope that this treatment of the data will satisfy those whose work brings into focus the individual, a perspective which is essential to the work of the therapeutic communities and to many other professionals treating troubled children. Naturally, in order to preserve her anonymity, we have changed Siobhan's name and other details.

The research reader, more concerned with groups, with outcomes and whether or not results are replicable, should not confuse our presentation of this subjective material with a lack of objectivity in our scrutiny of Caldecott. On the contrary, we have been very critical of some aspects of the Community's work, particularly its relative isolation from the families of the children it shelters. What is more, we hope that the Community will learn from the research and that plans will be implemented to remedy the weaknesses identified. Residential care must adapt and improve if it is to survive and we hope that this study will inform Caldecott's planning for the future.

For Siobhan too we hope for good outcomes, that she will be more settled, more robust and have more insight into her situation. As she is articulate and intelligent, she has better life chances than most in her situation. But we cannot hope for too much. Caldecott had much ground to cover in improving Siobhan's outlook, not least the confused family relationships, the trauma of abuse and her experience of being shunted around several unsatisfactory home and care settings. In the coming pages, we take a critical look at the care offered to Siobhan while she was at the Community and in the 12 months after she left.

Let us see how she and the Caldecott Community have developed over the four years we have been visiting them. We begin this task by learning a little more about Siobhan through an essay she prepared for us entitled 'My Life Story'.

,,

My life story

I was born in Queen Mary's hospital, Sidcup at 6 a.m. on 18th April. I then moved to Dublin in Ireland. My mum looked after myself and my four brothers reasonably well but my dad was an alcoholic and used to treat us badly. My mum had to suddenly go into hospital because of her kidneys, and because my dad was unable to look after us we all went into an orphanage in Dublin run by nuns. I don't have many memories of it but I hear it was horrible. My dad then kidnapped us and took us to Chislehurst in England and made every one of us wards of court. My mum finally came out of hospital and came over to England.

My mum and dad got back together again and things were going smoothly, until my dad started drinking again and they split up and my mum went back to Ireland. He then moved us all to a house in Catford. He got a girlfriend called Noreen Innis. Then my dad started sexually abusing me. Nobody knew about it. I was too scared to tell Noreen or my brothers. After a while my mum started to come and visit us, and she used to take us out on trips. I was even too scared to tell her.

My dad got rid of Noreen and my mum and dad made up yet again and we all moved to my nan's (on my dad's side) flat. My dad was still sexually abusing me without anybody knowing. My mum and dad split up again, so I lived some place with my dad but I can't remember where. My mum got court custody for us all and we all went to live in a flat with her. My brother Kurt was a daddy's boy (and still is) and ran away and went to my dad's house where he was living in Catford with Noreen again, and gave him the key to my mum's. A couple of nights later my dad came to the flat at about 3 a.m. and tried to kidnap us all again but didn't get very far so he beat up my mum instead. A few days later my mum and all of us (except Kurt who was still at my dads) went to my dad's house to try and get back the key but we didn't succeed so he beat us up. We had to go to a women's refuge in Bromley.

After a couple of years my mum got herself a boyfriend called Nick. He was quite a nice bloke. Then we moved to a council house in Bromley Common. Eventually I told my mum and Nick about my dad sexually abusing me and I had to go and see Dr Hirschi in Guy's Hospital. Then my brother Kurt moved in with us. Then he also started sexually abusing me. I built up the courage and told my mum and Nick about this after about six months. Kurt was put in a lock up at that time but I don't know whether it was for sexually abusing me or not, but it should have been. Then my brother Barry started to get involved in drugs and was staying out all night. He was put into a children's home called Bathwick in Farnborough.

Shortly after we moved to St. Johns Road in Farnborough, about five minutes away from Bathwick. At that time both my grandparents (on my mums side) died three weeks in between each other and my mum was going back and forth to Ireland. Then my mum and Nick split up and that was the end of Nick and we never saw him again. It was quite a shame because I quite liked him. Then none other than (brother) Adrian started to misbehave so shortly after he was put into care. So then it was just my mum, myself and Nigel. But Kurt lived there most of the time still sexually and physically abusing me, and used to come home drunk in the early hours of the morning and smash up the house.

All the stress got too much for my mum and she went into Farnborough Hospital. Nigel and I were put with foster parents in Chidingstone. We went on holiday to Rye with some students and hated it so asked to come back. When we got back to the foster parent she was worried that Nigel and I were going to run away so she phoned social services. We were supposed to go into a children's home in Dymchurch but it just so happened that that day my two aunts came over from Ireland. We went back to Ireland and stayed for about a month.

When my mum was well enough to come out of hospital me and Nigel went home. Shortly after my mum and I were arguing non-stop so it got too much and by January-February I asked to come into care. Nigel and I went to a children's home in Bromley. Nigel only stayed for a little while then he got ill and went into hospital. When he came out he went to foster parents. I was a bit annoyed that we had got split up. I got expelled from school. In July, although reluctant at first, I came to Caldecott. I went to the South of France for two weeks in August.

Part Two
History

The founding of Caldecott

The residential centre that Siobhan entered has a long and distinguished history. It is impossible in the context of a wider study to capture all of the elements of Caldecott's background. There are other texts that do this very well, not least the works of Elizabeth Lloyd and Margaret Stirling and the general context is also well covered in the writings of Parker, Ward, Pinchbeck and Hewitt and others. What we can achieve in this and following sections is to convey an impression of the principal themes underpinning the Community's development, both in the last 80 years and, no doubt, in the future.

For the first 60 years of its existence, its history was inexorably entwined with the life of one of its co-founders, Leila Rendel. 'Miss Leila' enjoyed two abiding loves, one for children and the other for hats. She never missed an opportunity to buy a hat or to help a child, indeed, these activities were often combined. Leila Rendel was fortunate to be born into a prosperous upper middle class London family but she eschewed the life of wealthy, ineffective gentility of a lady, preferring to bounce about a local gymnasium and to train as a PT teacher.

Leila Rendel and the co-founder of Caldecott, Phyllis Potter, grew up in the liberal, blue-stocking world of London intelligentsia. Here, as the nineteenth century drew to a close, the elegant drawing rooms of Liberal party supporters were noisy with social issues; with Ireland and the problems of home rule, with the Boer War, with inner-city poverty and decline and, particularly, with the plight of children and concerns with their education. These were linked to questions about national efficiency which the Boer War had cruelly exposed.

The problems of the London poor were not new but increasing emphasis upon education had highlighted deprivations. The London School Board reports of the time frequently commented on the poor physical condition of many young children attending schools. Mary Taber in Charles Booth's study *Life and Labour of the People of London* comments 'puny, pale faced, scantily clad and badly shod, these small and feeble folk may be found sitting limp and chill on the school benches in the poorer parts of London'. The School Board committee of 1889 suggested that one in eight children arrived at school habitually underfed. So, although England and Wales were late in the race to provide compulsory education, they were among the first countries in Europe to try to meet the wider needs of school children, particularly in food, clothing and medical care. Thus, legislation was introduced in 1907 to allow local authorities to spend rate money providing school meals and in 1908 the medical inspection of all school children became compulsory.

The Egerton Commission which reported in 1889 was primarily concerned with blind and deaf children, but also highlighted the problems of the less able child in schools and the need for special provisions. Later legislation thus paid attention to children who were handicapped, delicate or difficult and to those who could not cope with normal schooling. A host of voluntary organisations sought to address such needs. It was in this context that Leila Rendel and her colleague Phyllis Potter established the Caldecott Community in 1911 as a nursery school for the children of mothers who worked in a local matchbox factory.

Founding mothers

Leila Rendel was born in 1882. Her mother was the daughter of Kegan Paul, the publisher, and her father was the son of Sir Alexander Rendel, a civil engineer. The restless London scene prior to the First World War hardly gave much scope for women and the normal destinations did not appeal to Leila. During adolescence she attended the Chelsea College of Physical Education where she trained as a physical training teacher and she later worked for the Board of Education as a Junior Inspector.

However, more influential on Leila's career than PT training was the stimulation provided by her wealthy family and friends. She assiduously cultivated these contacts and was adept at persuading many of them to support her quest to put right that which she thought to be wrong. For example, the first president of the Caldecott Council in 1914 was HRH Princess Louise. Politicians, shipping magnates and even academics gave support to her work as, much later, did the Brabourne family by providing accommodation at Mersham-le-Hatch. Such patronage is evident in the Caldecott culture today and marks the Community apart from other residential child-care centres in England.

What sort of a woman was Leila Rendel? She was, by any standards, a charismatic leader and consequently was full of contradictions. Elizabeth Lloyd who has a long association with the Community described Leila Rendel as a 'lover of humanity and above all of children and young people. Leila was a born educator, courageous and far seeing, unafraid, seldom abashed and totally unselfconscious. She was also autocratic, sometimes too demanding yet curiously humble, always ready to listen'. Leila Rendel could both inspire and constrain and her presence in the Community is still felt today, too much so for some people's liking.

Of equal significance in these early days was Phyllis Potter, born in 1886 in South Kensington. She was the daughter of a wealthy ship owner. After leaving school she had trained at Selly Oak Theological College for a role as a Sunday School teacher. It was while she was running a nursery class at Whitefield's Tabernacle in the Tottenham Court Road that she first met Leila Rendel. Ever radical, Leila and Phyllis were both members of Webb's national committee, an association of vociferous do-gooders. Phyllis is particularly remembered as a reformer and pioneer, vigorously putting forward her views. Margaret Stirling describes her as 'brimming with dramatic energy and creative imagination'.

It is difficult to imagine how two such evidently powerful people managed to work harmoniously side by side for as many years as they did. Daisy Campbell, another long time member of staff, wrote, 'Leila Rendel and Phyllis Potter were a charming couple, so different in many ways but each complemented the other.' Although there is scant evidence of any hierarchy at Caldecott over the years, Phyllis Potter was clearly much in command: many comment on her qualities as a natural leader with a warmth of personality and a tremendous sense of drama. This sharing of senior roles has been an intermittent feature of Caldecott over the last 80 years and when taken with the absence of any obvious managerial structure, has been more of a strength than a weakness. There are many checks and balances on development at the Community and, unlike other major residential centres, organisational preoccupations have seldom been allowed to cast a shadow over child-care concerns.

Sadly the partnership of the first founding mothers came to an uneasy end. By 1931 Phyllis Potter had become increasingly High Church and she felt that the Caldecott Community should be run on a sectarian basis. Leila Rendel was not convinced. She saw value in setting aside a room for a chapel where all children, whether Catholics, Jews or Protestants would gather for prayers on Sundays. Conflict simmered and in 1932, when the Community moved to the Mote near Maidstone, Phyllis Potter left, creating a gulf that many thought could not be filled.

It seems that several people were asked by Leila Rendel to join her as co-director but all turned it down feeling that the task was too awesome and that Phyllis Potter could not be replaced. The task eventually fell to Ethel Davies, another wealthy heiress. Born in Liverpool in 1897, Ethel Davies's childhood was difficult since her parents were seldom on speaking terms. Perhaps these experiences stood her in good stead for her future life in the Community where her skill with children, especially with disturbed adolescent girls, was soon appreciated. Gradually a close and creative partnership between Leila Rendel and Ethel Davies developed, a harmonious relationship that lasted for more than 40 years and was only ended by Leila's death. Margaret Stirling described the relationship as 'the great strength of the Community'.

These three were the main actors on the stage of the Community's early history but the supporting cast consisted of many dedicated women who also devoted the whole of their working lives. Elizabeth Lloyd joined Caldecott in 1936 and remained for 35 years, Roma Easton stayed for 40 years. Kathleen Syer, who taught crafts, carpentry and weaving from just after the First World War did not retire until the mid 1950s. Ruth Rowson, an artist, started her association with Leila Rendel and Phyllis Potter at the Community's first home in St. Pancras and kept up the connection for over 50 years. Betty Hillyer remained for 42 years and Ethel Davies stayed until her retirement in 1972.

It was, evidently, a matriarchal society. Save the occasional carpenter, gardener or estate manager, no man was appointed to a caring task until Simon Rodway's arrival in 1951. The Community has been directed by men for the last 15 years and two-thirds of the residents are now boys but even today Caldecott does not seem to have succumbed to the patriarchy and male values which characterise much residential child-care. But the female values instilled in the life of the Community were those of the Edwardian marginalised middle-class. For many of these women, Caldecott offered a glimpse at another world. Many had never done any domestic chores before and few would have come into contact with troubled children or with truancy and delinquency. The Community was as much for adults as it was for children.

In many ways, Simon Rodway's arrival - as an unpaid care worker - marked a watershed in the life of the Community as it shifted towards a less gender-specific, more professional, fee-paying service with more clearly defined methods. In the estimation of some, several of the women stayed well past their prime and they departed together, causing considerable problems for the Community. James King, who became the director in 1968 on the death of Leila Rendel writes, 'A vote of no confidence in the directors was narrowly defeated. More staff left and as the old staff were quite irreplaceable, gaps opened everywhere. The difference in calibre between the old and the new staff was impossible to reconcile. I was just thankful to be inheriting a badly leaking ship rather than the pride of the fleet. We survived but it was a close run thing'.

Nonetheless, many aspects of Leila Rendel and Phyllis Potter's legacy endure. The importance of the great and the good in supporting the Community remains a feature of their work, though today most of the funds come from the local authorities that send the children. Until the recent retirement of James King, the idea of co-directors has continued, although the last incumbents were men. Possibly because of this management structure, some gap between the directors and the care workers is still apparent, as we shall see in later parts of this book. The financial insecurity of a voluntary organisation continues to be a feature and, although the Community has resided in a great Adam house near Ashford since 1947, the problem of tenure that marked the early years of Caldecott's life is once more a factor. We come back to these issues later; first let us consider the roots of the Community's approach to children.

Daily life

'We never had any theories', said Ethel Davies towards the end of her long association with Caldecott. Margaret Stirling agreed, 'Leila and Ethel endeavoured to follow where children led, dealing with their daily development and with crises according to the inspiration of the moment. We noted consequent failures and our successes for future guidance'. Leila Rendel put it another way, 'I believe in just sitting on the wall and soaking up the best that is around'.

However, by scrutinising the children's files, from talking to ex-residents and examining the writings of staff, some early influences become apparent. Maria Montessori's principles emphasising self-development and freedom were certainly attractive to the founders and among the gifts recorded in the first report is an entire set of Montessori Teaching Apparatus. Whether the degree of freedom suitable for the Italian young was applicable to London children became a subject of considerable debate. Nonetheless, the value of a method which could be used with both the less gifted and the child of normal intelligence was eagerly grasped and, unlike many other residential centres established at the beginning of the 20th century, at least there was a rational basis for the day-to-day work.

The early days of the Community were experimental and good ideas were not always found to be practicable. For example, parents were encouraged to make frequent visits and to feel part of the Community but its movement between several sites before and during the Second World War taken with its increasing distance from the St Pancras area and the homes of the children hindered these links. Even today, when research and legislation make access and contact between parents and absent children a necessity, the Community's performance in this respect is poor.

Each of the seven homes of the Community has been spartan and the atmosphere a little chilly. Sir Wilfred Stokes, the first honorary treasurer of Caldecott, felt bound to say, 'It must not be thought that there is any tendency to turn the children into young ladies or young gentlemen. There are no luxuries. All shared in scrubbing and other housework, and it is never forgotten that education is a preparation for a life of toil.' Whether the staff at Caldecott would have agreed with that assertion is debatable but certainly the ideal of genteel poverty, of high moral values and low costs pressed hard upon everyone. On the other hand, the availability of books, the presence of pictures and a willingness to participate in other aspects of cultural life have set the Community apart from other centres for deprived children.

Life may have been haphazard but the children were provided with security and stability. This became increasingly important as the proportion of children coming from disturbed homes grew. As we shall see, by the 1930s, deprived, maladjusted and even delinquent children were pressing for shelter. Ironically, efforts to meet the child's need for continuity meant many new experiments and endless adaptations. Many from the outside world testified to the vitality of the Caldecott Community at this period.

Who should benefit from these experiments? Leila Rendel deliberately selected relatively intelligent children, a decision which led to charges of elitism which have stuck to the Community ever since. Her aim was essentially preventive, to rescue intelligent children from disintegrating homes early enough to prevent subsequent maladjustment and possible delinquency. Most children took time to adapt to this sudden expectation that they should acquire knowledge but once they began to advance and they were freed from the anxieties and fears of the past, it was difficult to envisage them returning home. Stays at Caldecott were, as a consequence, long. Each child was encouraged to develop in its own way and at its own pace. Teacher/pupil ratios were generous and plenty of time was allocated to creative work, drama and music. Although they are commonplace in the curriculum today, art, dance, drama, mime and music were innovative and unusual during the 1930s. The children did as much as they could; acting, telling stories, singing and dancing. The event of the week was the Sunday sing-song in which each child had to get up from the floor and walk out to specially chosen music.

In the 1930s, Desirée Martin was brought in to teach the Dalcroze method of eurhythmics. Other influential educational ideas, not necessarily congruent with one another, were introduced and came to bear upon the life of the Community. These included the Dalton and Froebel methods of teaching. Unfortunately such pragmatism attracted critics and, although supported by other pioneers, usually highly opinionated people intolerant of any divergent views, the Caldecott Community was often dismissed 'as a place where children ran around'.

Other influences can be found. Leila Rendel had a lifelong association with Gordonstoun where she was a governor. Its founder, Kurt Hahn, had considerable bearing on Caldecott's development: ten Caldecott children won scholarships to Gordonstoun and one girl was despatched to Hahn's centre in Germany. The values of an outdoor, frugal life so emphasised by Hahn at Gordonstoun appealed to Leila Rendel, as did the communing with nature and the value of silent periods of contemplation and reflection for children. Particularly influential was the idea of La Grande Passion and children were encouraged to find recreation and fulfilment in a wide variety of ways. Kurt Hahn believed that, 'The secret of education lay not in probing into the unconscious mind or into incidence of infant experience or in any special technique of instruction but in providing a healthy structure'. The pursuit of individual interests was certainly popular but another feature borrowed from Gordonstoun, that of compulsory early morning runs for both boys and girls followed by a cold shower, rested less easily with other aspects of the Caldecott regime.

Despite the crisis which led to Phyllis Potter's departure, religion played an important role in the life of the Community. Leila Rendel believed in the 'divine purpose of the work' and she laid down some very firm guidelines on the Community's religious life:

> It shall provide for children of any creed, nationality or social class who, by reason of parental death, sickness, divorce, separation or other inadequacy, or through illegitimacy were deprived of the secure and loving family environment regarded as essential for emotional and personal development.

This eclectic and tolerant attitude is still stressed at the Community today, almost by necessity, as residents have become increasingly multicultural. Benign though the regime at Caldecott was, Leila Rendel eschewed the freedom of many progressive schools such as Summerhill and Dartington. As with any community, disciplinary measures were necessary. Caldecott had a policy of outlawing physical punishment; however, older children were known to administer slaps to the younger ones. As a general rule, offenders were dealt with by removing them from the group. Margaret Stirling writes,

> Children who were naughty were placed in isolation for a time, thus a small boy spent his free afternoon tethered to a gooseberry bush from which he had previously stolen all the unripe gooseberries. A small girl of two who had been so impossibly grumpy that she was finally wheeled in her pram into a field and left by herself under a large oak tree, she was later seen laughing and chuckling to herself at the cows who had come over to see who it was invading their field. One very wet day a child became so impossible that she finally was put into a mackintosh and turned outside. She returned from her drenching a changed child and quite happy again.

Other controls included those of social duties which were given as a reparation for offences and consisted of polishing shoes, cutlery or extra housework and the depriving of the child of free time.

Conclusions

Many aspects of the Community's early development are apparent in the work of Caldecott today. The focus on education, the attention to spiritual needs of the child, the concern with the cultural world of the residents are features of the Community, as Siobhan's story testifies. Similarly, the difficulty of fashioning a coherent intervention in the face of a rapidly changing resident population also endures. All of these values have to be captured and transmitted in the ethos of the Community for nowhere are they clearly written down.

Other aspects of Leila Rendel and Phyllis Potter's pioneering efforts are manifest. The failure to get around the practical difficulties of involving remote families in the Community is an issue we return to later in this book. Interestingly, the charge of elitism is still heard, although the children sheltered at Caldecott when Siobhan arrived were far more difficult than those selected from the back streets of Kings Cross by the earnest Miss Leila. The rivalry between the progressive schools and therapeutic communities continues even though nowadays some form of cooperation is vital for their survival.

If we think of the Caldecott's development as a series of layers which form the basis of the work with children, what best characterises the contribution of the founding mothers? Simon Rodway has described Leila Rendel's philosophy as having three elements. First, children are given a pattern and significance to their lives which involves finding a reasonable balance between freedom and order. Second, emphasis is given to continuity of care, in filling gaps in a child's life - intellectually and emotionally. Third, the Community tries to recognise each child as an individual; unlike many other residential centres there is no herding of residents and children's rights, only recently introduced into community homes and boarding schools, have long been a priority at Caldecott.

In his Diamond Jubilee address to the Community, Rodway states that Caldecott stands for 'honesty, integrity, simplicity, inspiration and courage'. To these qualities we can add the different contributions of James King, Margaret Stirling and Michael Jinks who, as we shall see, have added new layers to Caldecott's foundations. In this study, we shall try to highlight other influences that can be brought to bear upon the Community's development; influences that will give the work a congruity with new movements in child-care, with increased professionalism, the growing reliance on market forces and the new found emphasis upon research and training.

Caldecott can build on its firm foundations. The ideas fashioned eight decades ago still echo around the Community which Siobhan joined in 1990. When it was established, Leila Rendel and Phyllis Potter would probably have hoped that the need for residence for London children would have evaporated. Certainly, the youngsters they took into their care in the early days would be safely sheltered at home in the 1990s but new categories of need have emerged, a feature of work with vulnerable children that, sadly, is unlikely to change in the foreseeable future.

Children at Caldecott in the 40s and 50s

There is an annual reunion of children who have left Caldecott. Numbers change from year to year but at least 50 attend the day which includes a church service, a meal and a party. The oldest participants are in their mid-fifties and most are over 30 years of age. Going back and meeting those who know us in our childhood is never easy. As one of the Community *alumni* put it:

> You cannot hide at these occasions. Everybody knows who you really are. I may be all dressed up but if I start with my airs and graces then somebody is bound to say, 'Come off it Jenny, it's us you're talking to!'

Nonetheless, year after year graduates return to the Community. Some have been helped by Caldecott since leaving, especially the 20 or so who each year benefit from the Leila Rendel Fund or from pastoral support from the Committee that oversees this bequest. Many are still in regular touch with a member of staff to whom they formed a special attachment. A group are regular visitors to Elizabeth Lloyd, and Simon Rodway is endlessly rushing about London suburbs supporting ex-Caldecott pupils and their children, including the 18 to whom he is a godparent. Barbara Watt, James and Tessa King, as several other names of Caldecott staff are frequently mentioned as having recently supported people who were at the Community many years ago. Several of the longer serving managers at Caldecott today also provide voluntary after-care.

We could have picked any of the leavers attending the reunion to interview. As a group they are not typical of all graduates because the majority of leavers have never been back to the Community. No single person could be said to be representative, but we felt it important to report at least one of their stories so as to capture the flavour of the Community 30 years ago and to get some indication of the long-term outcomes for children.

Trevor Newington entered Caldecott in circumstances commonplace during the 1950s and, as we shall see later, commonplace today. He was displaying behavioural difficulties. His problems did not warrant consideration for a place in a reformatory school but he was testing the patience of the child guidance clinic and local school. Forty years on, as a wealthy managing director of his own building company, his situation marks him apart from most others he meets at the reunion. We have not chosen his case because, materially at least, it turned out well. Indeed, driving to meet him, one of the Committee members of the Leila Rendel Fund enthusiastically pointed out the homes of graduates who were continuing to have difficulty '.... there's Michael's house, he's having a terrible time at the moment .... in the Scrubs after refusing to go on an Alcoholics Anonymous programme as part of a Probation Order .... we are giving his wife £50 a week towards housekeeping' or 'Henry, tragic case ... in and out of hospital, a schizophrenic ... he manages well when he takes his medication but needs our help in between times'.

Trevor Newington may not be typical but he does provide an eloquent description of the circumstances that got him to Caldecott and his memories of Community life can help with an understanding of the situation and outcomes of children in Caldecott today.

> I was born as the Second World War was coming to an end. My parents came to Liverpool as the war got under way, they were evacuated from Shanghai by the Japanese and arrived in England rootless. My father was English, but I don't know where from. My mother was half Sicilian and half Chinese. Father was in the army, an interpreter; they both spoke at least three languages but not the same ones as each other. Communication has always been a problem for us although as you can hear, I'm fairly articulate.
>
> I am a classic deprived child really, from the bottom of a deprived family. But it wasn't always like that for them. My parents

are the products of affluentVictorian society. My grandfather was a chartered accountant and my parents were very cultured. As well as the languages and the travel there was music. My father played the piano and the flute. One of my regrets in life is that none of these talents have been passed on to me.

We were in Liverpool until I was seven. We were a big family, I had eight brothers and a sister, the oldest is now 61 and the youngest is 39. At 49, I am the third to last. We were deprived in a physical sense. When I went to Caldecott it was the first time I had my own toothbrush and I never had my own underwear before then. But the physical disadvantages were as nothing compared to the emotional problems. Father came from strict Brethren stock and I suppose he was unable to convey his feelings. I never sat on his knee, I never climbed into bed with my parents. When I compare that to my children's experiences today. My mother was better than father but, although she was brilliant with babies, she was terrible with toddlers.

There were pockets of caring at home. My brothers and sister and I all cared deeply for each other but we were never close. Having said that, when I was at Caldecott I was very homesick for my brothers; not for home, just for my brothers, I missed them. Especially in the second and third terms.

We moved to Luton when I was seven and by eight I was beginning to cause trouble. Everybody thought I was following in brother Gerald's footsteps; he was taken away to Colomendy camp (a residential centre for disturbed boys) when we were in Liverpool. I couldn't do anything at home except cook. (Trevor is a very good cook today). Otherwise my self esteem was none existent, I was worthless as far as my father was concerned. I got caught stealing money from a dentist and then I was seeing child guidance and next I was off to Caldecott. I went under the 1944 *Education Act*, I think. I went for care and protection and because child guidance said I required boarding education and my parents couldn't pay. I was the only one in our family to go away like this.

On arrival at Caldecott, a range of possible outcomes were available to Trevor. He had quite a lot going for him; he was clever, attractive and, while his home life was unsatisfactory, he had a family. Trevor also brought with him a basket full of misfortune; he was rootless, emotionally deprived, he had low self esteem and was delinquent. Ask him today as he stands in his company director suit next to his Jaguar car with personal number plate outside a house set in several acres of land what would have happened had Caldecott not intervened and he answers, 'a downward spiral of crime, drugs and prison', the fate of brother Gerald.

Based on the evidence we have, we cannot say with any certainty whether Caldecott did contribute to Trevor's good fortune. We can be sure that, in retrospect, he enjoyed the experience; he describes it as heaven for the first few months; the first experience of childhood; 'the first time I had any sense of belonging'. At the Community, he acquired a family of which he is still a part today. Indeed, so close is Trevor to his Caldecott roots, his wife feels almost excluded and pushed out from the group of ex-residents and staff with whom her husband keeps in touch.

> I have been very fortunate having my Caldecott family. It's very difficult to compress into a few hours' talking the feeling of happiness I experienced during this period of my childhood. It opened a whole new horizon to me. It was a wonderful feeling of a childhood that had not existed before then. If you have read Arthur Hailey's *Roots* you will understand that I think of Caldecott as my roots.
>
> It also gave me skills although I threw away my last year at school. I took my CSEs at secondary school but was thought too rebellious for Ashford College so they packed me off to Harvey Grammar in Folkestone. I enjoyed myself there, especially playing cricket and came away with only two O-levels. But I wasn't put off school and still have an affection for the ones I've been to.
>
> I don't want to give the impression it was all marvellous because it wasn't. There were times when I was in the depths of despair, like all children. And I was a little sod; I gave the staff the run-around. They were a very committed group of people. They stuck at it and they didn't earn much for all they took from us. In fact, there were times that Caldecott was so broke they didn't get paid anything at all. Now, when I look back, there are no members of staff I don't look back on without affection and esteem. They were saints getting on with what they had to get on with. … No, I didn't see much of Miss Leila, she never had much to do with the boys but her influence was always there.
>
> I kept in touch with my family when I was away. For a start it was not 52 weeks a year care, so we mostly went home during holidays. But every Sunday was letter writing day and every week

I sent a letter to my mother and, to give her due, every Wednesday one came back. Even people without parents had to write to somebody. .... My parents only visited Caldecott twice and I was devastated when once I found out they had driven past the front door without coming in to see me. I was in hospital at the time after a fall and they went to Folkestone and didn't even think of me on the way!

In the end I went back home. It was just assumed that this would happen, you went at 15, although a few were moved on early. The leaving was played down and like every end of term it was a bit of an anticlimax. And you were not encouraged to come back for a while, I think there was a rule that you couldn't go to a reunion for at least two years. People were encouraged to make their own way, to cut the traces. At that time there was no official after care although I had Simon Rodway and the girls had Marion Kidd. Simon has been a wonderful help to me and is godfather to my son but never in the 30 years since leaving have I stayed at Caldecott again. Other ex-Caldecott people came and stayed when I was there, it would also have been good for me.

I went home but it wasn't much better than before. My father was very dictatorial still and I had changed. I had been through a system and had achieved deputy head prefect at school. Caldecott had given me autonomy and respect and my parents could not accept this independence. My father didn't like people with opinions, unless they were opinions he shared!

I took an apprenticeship and did well. And I stayed for three years at home until one my brothers came back after being deported from Kenya and dumped in England. We shared a house for three years, then I took digs in Harpenden for 12 months until I married in 1969.

Given that my brothers and sister didn't go to Caldecott, mostly they didn't leave home at all, you could ask whether I have done any better because of my time in Ashford. It's hard to say. One brother, Desmond, died and another, Gerald, disappeared off the face of the earth 25 years ago. My sister married an army officer and did very well. The eldest brother, who was my father's favourite and received a private education, Victor, did nothing with his life and became long-term unemployed. Two have become teachers and two have retired, one after an operation that went wrong. I don't know what you make of this. Am I doing well? Yes and No.

I was separated from my first wife in September 1984. I have now married again and have two children aged four years and six months and I have a stepdaughter of 21. The apprenticeship and professional qualifications I gained all stood me in good stead and over 20 years I have built the business up. I wouldn't say it to most people but as nobody will know my real identity from this interview I will say that I am very successful in what I do. I have a set of people values that work. Caldecott taught you that. A group of 15 or 16 adolescent boys, all from different walks of life, all with different abilities and disabilities living together for 24 hours a day, you just had to learn to get along with each other. That's been good for me in my business.

After I separated from my ex-wife, I started to live with my current wife and her daughter. There were no children from my first marriage but I don't know if this made any difference to the outcome, I don't know if it ever would have worked with Beverley. I never felt married with her. Now we have two children aged four years and one as well as my stepdaughter who is 21. I want my childhood at Caldecott to be part of their childhood. I wish I could bottle up some of the experiences and pass them on; some of the Christmas parties, the holly wreath with the apples and the candles; meeting the Duke of Edinburgh at Buckingham Palace to get my award, the woodwork teacher, the simple beauty of the place. All this I would like to pass on to my children.

Am I happy? ....Yes, I think so. I am well balanced and I get on as well as anybody with my fellow man. This is particularly so in the last five years and obviously my family is very important to me.

Have I been lucky? Not in the sense you might think. Business is a skill and the one thing you cannot be is lucky. Blessed, yes. I am blessed in the relationships I have got and have had.

Conclusion

Children stay long at Caldecott but the experience only represents a tiny proportion of their lives. Trevor says that 'illness of the mind takes a long time to cure' and as he enters his fiftieth year, having made an apparent success of his life, he still seeks some support from the Community. When we ask whether he is happy, Trevor hesitates, suggesting that however a treatment intervention is framed, there will always be more to do.

For all its shortcomings, and in the coming pages we identify many, the fact that Caldecott stays in touch with so many of its graduates is remarkable. Much of Caldecott's involvement is based upon the special relationships formed by philanthropic members of staff with their charges. Such a level of involvement was the norm before and just after the Second World War but, while it is still a feature of Caldecott life, it tends to be frowned upon today. That Trevor and others have benefited in some way from a special relationship is beyond doubt.

The preceding pages demonstrate the sense of belonging good residential care can instil into vulnerable children. Indeed, Trevor can still remember the Caldecott Charter and Leila Rendel chanting at the beginning of every term:

> This household is a Community.
> And the members of this household are ...

after which the names of all children and staff would be read out.

Trevor's words also hint at historical continuities in the life of Caldecott. The maintenance of family links but the virtual exclusion of parents from Caldecott itself; the strain placed upon young staff; the premature departure of extremely difficult children; the emphasis upon education and the attempt to get Caldecott children into local mainstream schools; all these features of the Community in the 1950s exist today. There is a tendency to see weaknesses in residential care as recent inventions, possibly the result of a lack of resource. In fact, many of the deficiencies and strengths of this system have a long history and, while the Community still struggles to make ends meet, compared to 30 years ago it is very well endowed.

Caldecott is changing. Hearing about life there in the 1950s we are struck by the simplicity of its ministry. The Charter to build up a sense of belonging and the letter writing to maintain family links represented straightforward remedies to difficult problems in residential care. Today, the service has become much more complex. We know much more about the children and their needs, far more has been written about treatment and now there are studies such as this providing evidence on what happens before, during and after a sojourn at Caldecott. Nonetheless, any future developments at Caldecott must be made with these historical continuities in mind. We shall consider these further with a look at Caldecott since the Second World War.

Caldecott since the war

As in so much else in the lives of disadvantaged children, the Second World War proved a turning point in the fortunes of the Caldecott Community as it did in special education generally. The clients began to change, with the more difficult, more delinquent and considerably more insecure being thrust forward for services. In the early days, few would have quarrelled with the simple ideology of Caldecott, but as time passed considerably more was needed and not all change was welcome.

While many Communities and schools were radical in their internal arrangements, fashioning all sorts of self-governing units with varying degrees of shared responsibility, those caught up in the special schools movement were frequently less than forward looking. Neither critical of the social and economic forces working to impoverish families and create their clients nor expressing much concern over the indifference of government to act on the dismal educational and welfare experience of the vast majority of children, it quickly became an inward looking system about which the outside world knew and cared very little.

The Second World War changed all this. The fireside chats of J B Priestly and Donald Winnicott, the latter a great friend of Caldecott, heightened awareness of the needs of separated children. Parents clustered around the radios in Anderson shelters had little alternative but to listen to these child-care lectures. Also influential was the mass evacuation of children from the big cities and their arrival in the gin and tonic belts of the Home Counties, into the beautiful, smug English villages and cathedral towns of the travel books. Suddenly families in the safe Shires, whose idea of hardship was cook's day off, found themselves with the separated, poor, under-fed, desperate children from the inner cities. The manifest needs of these waifs and refugees produced a storm of indignation that so many children should be so badly looked after. Meeting their needs was not the responsibility of charity, it was the job of government and, as in so much else, government had failed.

The strictures of Leila Rendel and other pioneers on the inadequate provision made for children at risk suddenly became a national concern. Child care was clearly unsatisfactory and formidable English ladies, like rhinoceroses dressed in tweeds, made their way to Westminster. They frightened Winston Churchill more than the Luftwaffe; he made Clement Atlee see them, who, ever conciliatory, acquiesced in their demands for change. Many of our distinguished child care figures had their baptisms of fire as young women looking after evacuees.

The problems were severe and not only faced Caldecott. For example, Susan Isaacs estimated that two per cent of children involved in the evacuation would be unsuitable for foster homes on account of the nervous symptoms and difficult behaviour they displayed. She advocated that these would be best cared for in small group homes of 10 to 15 children. The experience of South Wales, Oxford and other reception areas confirmed her fears. Maurice Bridgeland comments,

> The evolution of child care, of 'special' education, of therapy was vastly accelerated by the war, indeed one wonders whether new approaches to the problem would ever have become nationally accepted if the war had not made maladjustment a national issue. There were few signs before the war that the lone voices of pioneer individuals would ever be swelled to a national chorus. However, such was the impetus given to the recognition of the needs of the maladjusted by wartime conditions that there is little in the subsequent development of special education that does not stem from this period.

The war had other effects, not all beneficial. The evacuation showed that foster care, the placement of children in alternative families, seemed to work. It was a message not lost on the Home Office, the responsible government department. Foster care was cheap and the majority of children settled well. On the other hand, the minority of difficult children who could not cope in alternative families also achieved a salience. John Bowlby, Donald Winnicott, Anna Freud, Mia Kelmer Pringle all worked with children who presented as disturbed by separation and the war had taught everyone something of the traumas of being apart from loved ones. For children an omnipresent mother was key, particularly in the early years. Increasingly the work at the Paddington Clinic, the Tavistock and Maudesley Hospitals, initially so important to the development of the Caldecott Community, began to question the benefits of residential care and to criticise the child rescue philosophy. Leila Rendel herself contributed much to these discussions and helped orchestrate considerable political pressure through her Fabian Society contacts.

The great social changes came in the establishment of local authority structures for vulnerable children. Lady Allen of Hurtwood was a catalyst by her letter to *The Times* in 1944 which stated 'the social upheaval caused by the war has not only increased this army of unhappy children but presents the opportunity for transforming their conditions. The Committee of Enquiry set up under Dame Myra Curtis in 1945 highlighted a chaotic system in which deprived children received inadequate care from four different central authorities. Her findings still exercise enormous influence on our child care services. The committee made many radical recommendations, some of which were close to Leila Rendel's heart. From this point onwards, the main source of referrals to the Community would increasingly come from public bodies and not private families and, as a consequence, the State had a greater say in the affairs of voluntary organisations like Caldecott.

The Curtis Report had wide ranging effects. Local authority children's departments were created, training was given a high priority, the importance of the natural family and swift reunion was recognised as was the need for assessment of children's problems. In 1948, aided by a grant from the Nuffield Educational Trust, and armed with ideas from the University of Birmingham, Mia Kelmer-Pringle established at Caldecott the first Observation and Assessment Centre in the country. The Curtis Committee also severely criticised the quality of much residential provision, particularly when it was indifferent to residents' emotional and expressive needs. Children's legislation in 1948, 1969 and, most recently, 1989 have led to a greater stress on prevention, of using the natural family as a resource, keeping families together and on the flexible use of substitute care arrangements. Clearly, Caldecott has increasingly been pushed towards the more difficult child whom others are reluctant to shelter.

The creation of the children's departments within local authorities had lasting significance for residential care. As we shall see in later sections, demand for residential provision declined, and the larger voluntaries such as the National Childrens Home and Barnardos have practically withdrawn from the sector altogether. But, Caldecott, unlike many other residential settings had much going for it. A good relationship had been long established with London child guidance services and the Tavistock Clinic provided referrals. Kent and other home counties were also committed to Caldecott's work. Almost unique was the provision of good primary education for those at risk or too vulnerable to attend day school. It could also manage the difficulties of transition from primary to secondary school. Consequently, referrals and admissions continued to be drawn from both education and social services departments and numbers held up. But full order books seldom endure and can lull anyone into a false sense of security as the progressive and preparatory schools have recently found to their cost.

The Community had to adapt to survive. The wholesome mixed grain loaf beloved of Leila Rendel became a nutty fruit cake of acting out children and adolescents. When she died in March 1969 inexorable and uncomfortable changes were being forced not only on Caldecott but also on residential child care and special education as a whole. Hostility towards residential care was being given added authority by accumulating research, some stemming from the work of Mia Kelmer Pringle and Anna Freud who were erstwhile supporters of the Community. The studies of the Tizards and Michael Rutter also cast doubts. The special school system, although largely untroubled, also came under scrutiny and was subject to successive changes in the Warnock and Fish Reports.

Restructuring and consolidation

For all its strengths in adapting to the world changing about them, Caldecott had become marginal to much child-care by the time of Leila Rendel's death. While the founding mothers were pioneering in spirit, they had not kept up with changing attitudes and ideas; they were ill-suited to the challenges which faced the Community in the 1960s. By many accounts it became something of a curiosity. It was, in James King's words an emotionless place in which the ultimate sin was to show any attachment to the children. An ageing staff group was, like its mentor, highly committed to children but, unlike Leila Rendel and Ethel Davies, little informed by the growing body of knowledge in the area.

The 60s and 70s also saw changes in the behaviours, aspirations and lifestyles of residents and the younger adult carers. Leila Rendel's achievement in Maurice Bridgeland's words, 'of conserving the good things of her liberal Edwardian past', came under fire. Tinkling pianos beneath dazzling Adam ceilings and vistas down to the lake were past their sell by date. Jeans, cacophony, frenzied movement, above all sex, preoccupied most children over ten years of age. At the same time haunted faces of visiting social workers urged sensitivity to cultural integrity, to ethnic foods and agonised over gender issues.

It was into this environment that James King entered in 1961. Without his work and the contribution of Margaret Stirling who later joined him as co-director, the Community might well have faltered. Leila Rendel's death stunned Caldecott and prompted the retirement of older members of staff. It was difficult to find new recruits and those that came were frequently young, highly inexperienced but were prepared to challenge the principles upon which the daily functioning of the Community was based. Amid constant crisis management, King and Stirling restructured the Community eventually creating a model upon which broader developments in the 1980s could build.

Changes within

The first change was the establishment of family groups to replace the dormitory provision that had previously existed. The initial moves in this direction were crude; cubicles were erected within the existing sleeping quarters. But from this point onwards, Caldecott became something more than a special boarding school and the exalted 'therapeutic Community' (bestowed by the psychotherapist Clarence Wollen) became ever more likely. The family groups encouraged staff to share roles and work together thus providing the children with the continuities in adult support that had previously been a feature. Children were also encouraged to support each other and to form relationships. There was a practical dimension to these changes: the older breed of staff member who could be expected to stay long – sometimes too long – were replaced by 'adults', young people who viewed a short tenure of two or at most three years as their lifetime commitment to this work.

Devolved management to the family groups gave the directors more time to cope with other challenges. The behaviour of staff was frequently as problematic as that of the children. Graduates from the new universities were never likely to behave to the standards set down by the founding mothers and, in addition to difficulties arising from differences in perspective, more staff than ever were employed with a more equal balance between men and women. The children also posed new problems, testing boundaries as the Community sought to discover whom it could and could not look after.

Change outside

Any new internal arrangements would simply have been cosmetic had Leila Rendel's role as the powerhouse of the Community not been replaced. But instead of looking for a person, Caldecott decided to restructured its governing council. Instead of a group of dignitaries to grace the residential centre by association – the typical arrangement – a group of child-care, legal and financial professionals as well as others with good business acumen were gathered. While not employed by Caldecott, council members work for the Community in a variety of ways.

This arrangement has been extremely successful. It has helped provide financial stability to the Community and has been the catalyst for several of Caldecott's most recent and exciting developments, not least the introduction of a more sophisticated treatment regime, the erection of new purpose-built units, the opening of a training college and the commissioning of research, including that which led to this book. The council, through a series of sub-committees, links the Community with the outside world, provides external scrutiny of the daily life of the units and school and, most importantly, stops Caldecott lurching precipitately into untested policies, practice or treatments.

These fundamental changes in the Community's life came about during the stewardship of James King and Margaret Stirling. It is possible that their efforts saved Caldecott from extinction and their work had long standing benefits. They reawakened the emotional world of the Community, so that touching and 'hugs' – effectively banned in Rendel's day – became commonplace. Staff training, for example, in dealing with violent incidents became more common during this period and the successful attempts to get all secondary school children into mainstream education led to good relationships with teachers in the Ashford and Folkstone areas.

Recent advances

At the beginning of the decade, James King was joined as co-director by Michael Jinks from the Cotswold Community. Cotswold had been transformed in the 1960s from the worst sort of approved school for juvenile delinquents to a therapeutic community for difficult and disturbed adolescents. Its leader, Richard Balbernie, was highly respected for his work, although, like many other pioneers in this field, his thoughts were seldom committed to paper or tested by research. Jinks brought to Caldecott many of the ideas and traditions developed at Cotswold as well as several members of staff.

Caldecott's treatment programme should be evident from other parts of this book so we shall say little here about Michael Jinks's contribution, save that he has confirmed upon Caldecott the identity of a therapeutic community and has brought to the place other trappings of a specialised centre. These include a team of consultants, including the psychologist Philip Maggs, psychiatrist Elspeth Earle and psychotherapist David Challender, the language of the psychoanalytic tradition and an expectation that staff should read and learn about the approach.

Other steps forward have been achieved in the last 15 years. A proper curriculum and form structure - in short a full, inspected secondary school - has been integrated within the Caldecott campus. The opening of Lacton Hall, a purpose built unit for the younger disturbed child, marked the beginning of 52 week care in 1985. The financial organisation has been revamped allowing the Community to respond creatively to the increasing market forces operating within local authorities and to institute new initiatives such as the after-care programme for Caldecott leavers. Most of these developments receive some evaluation in the coming pages.

Conclusions

A glance at Caldecott in the years since the Second World War reveals continuity and change. The insecurity of place and funding continues to this day but the matriarchal society has been swept away to be replaced by a more democratic environment in which men and, more importantly, working-class staff (and children) freely find a place. The sharing of senior roles in the Community, a practice which marks Caldecott apart from all similar centres in the United Kingdom, will probably survive by necessity; the job of directing a large therapeutic centre now demands a wide range of skills. Unfortunately, as later sections of this book testify, it has not closed the gap between the top of the organisation and those working at the bottom. As in any history of residential care, our scrutiny has been as much about those running Caldecott and the tensions between them as it has about the children they look after.

Today, Caldecott is an established therapeutic community and is very much child focused, perhaps too much so as far as local authorities adhering to the principles of the *Children Act*, 1989 are concerned. Is this term a 'therapeutic community' one which Leila Rendel would have recognised? Probably not, but she would accord with the search for a treatment philosophy and would also recognise the salience achieved by education, a feature which again sets Caldecott apart from most other residential centres. Leila Rendel would also acknowledge the charge of elitism which endures to this day.

The founding mothers might sense continuity within the walls of Caldecott, but they would be perplexed by the changes outside. Much of this has been for the good, for example, in the day care services which today are sufficient to meet the needs of children that Caldecott once sheltered. These wider changes have meant that residential care has declined and only a few children who refuse to settle either at home or in other substitute care settings are thrust forward for a place at the Community. We doubt whether the founders would recognise these children or know how to muster the resources to look after them.

Since the Second World War, the expectations of the service provided by the Community have increased. More than ever before, Caldecott is in an economic market which highly influences the quality of care on offer. As following sections demonstrate, the Community has always adapted to the needs of children and it continues to draw on the patronage of the great and good to develop its service. But in modern parlance Caldecott is a provider and if it does not satisfy its purchasers, like many similar organisations, it will be doomed. The purchaser continues to be both education and social services departments in local authorities. At different points since the war either one or both of these departments has needed to call upon residence in order to complete its work and Caldecott has responded. Thus, while similar experimental ventures have fallen by the wayside, the momentum behind Caldecott's work has continued.

The Caldecott today is very different from the Community at the end of the Second World War. One fact alone is very telling. In 1950 there were 120 children and only 40 staff; today 80 children are supported by 150 adults. If we return to the metaphor of Caldecott's foundations as a series of layers, three have been identified. There is the commitment to education and to new ways of thinking about and supporting troubled children - a tradition started by the founding mothers. Then there is the family group organisation and the introduction of external checks and balance in the 1960s and 70s. Finally, there have been the improvements to the treatment regime and financial arrangements instituted in the last 15 years. Further developments will be needed if Caldecott is to keep pace with child care services and continue to provide a focus for thinking about the needs of severely troubled children.

The Caldecott campus

Over the years, the Community has moved from house to house, some grand and some less than grand. Its first home was humble, a small house in Cartwright Gardens in St Pancras. The interior was decorated with illustrations from the childrens' books of Randolph Caldecott – hence the name 'Caldecott'. Today the Community surrounds a mansion built in the 18th century by the celebrated architect, Robert Adam. At the outset Caldecott sheltered 13 children, today there are nearly 80.

Escaping Cartwright Gardens and the ravages of the Great War, the Community settled in Charlton Court, East Kent in 1917 only to be moved again in 1925 to Goffs Oak in Hertfordshire. Seven years later, Caldecott retreated back to Kent, this time to Mote near Maidstone. The Second World War once again caused disruption and the Community moved first to Oxford and then Dorset. It was not until 1947 that, thanks to the generosity of the Brabourne family, Caldecott was able to come back to Kent and reside in the Adam House illustrated in the drawings and photographs. Even today, however, the security and stability offered to the children contrasts with the uncertainty over funding and accommodation continuously faced by the governing council.

At first glance, the current home seems an unlikely place for a residential child care centre. Built for the Knatchbull family between 1762 and 1766, it was the first house designed by Robert Adam after a long sojourn in Italy. The grand symmetrical plan, the magnificent ceilings and the beautiful vistas over the lake and gardens belong more to the National Trust than social and educational services. Yet hidden within the main building are six separate living units each sheltering ten children, offices for the administrative, domestic and maintenance staff as well as facilities for the several specialist consultants employed by the Community.

In the grounds – in the old stables – there is a school large enough to take in most of the Caldecott children. Within the estate and in the surrounding villages are many houses used to accommodate staff and visitors. Half a mile away towards Folkestone, there is the Caldecott College, a large Victorian building recently redeveloped to meet identified gaps in effective training for residential social workers. A mile in the opposite direction along the same road there are two other living units; Lacton Hall which predominately houses adolescents and Lacton House which cares for young and very needy children.

Woodside, in which much of this book is set, is just one unit in the West wing of the Adam House. It has its own front door, kitchen, dining room, office and play room and a rather curious jumble of living and bedrooms spread between three floors. It is the antithesis of a local authority children's home but has the capacity to operate like one. Unlike its local authority counterpart, it can also draw on the resources of the administration, specialists, school and other living units within the Community.

In most respects, the other living units with the mansion are similar to Woodside. Lacton House, two miles away, is rather different. Purpose built in 1985, its architecture reflects the needs of troubled children and has been a great success. This has prompted the Community to plan several new living units which, eventually, will replace those currently in use in the mansion house. The first, Leopold Muller House is, at the time of writing, about to open.

Much of this development has both sprung from and is calling into question the future of the Adam House as the Caldecott's principal home. Unfortunately, Grade I listed buildings are not easily adapted to the needs of children and the increasing cost of restoring and maintaining the property – though shared with English heritage – is soaking up resources that might better be spent on residents. Moreover, as we shall see, parents more used to the dreary surroundings of a social services department sub-office are frequently intimidated by the grandeur of the current surroundings.

This said, any transition away from the mansion will be difficult. Adam's house has given Caldecott an identity – a slightly eccentric identity – but one which is known to many professionals in the world outside and, as the previous sections have illustrated, it also has special meaning for ex-residents. The Community also gives the Adam house a vitality that is seldom seen in grand piles and it would be sad to see the unpredictable screams of children replaced with the sombre devotions of National Trust volunteers.

Part Three
Children's circumstances

Children at Caldecott 1911-1990

The great Adam house has sheltered several hundred children since it was turned over to the Community and in its previous settings it admitted many more, adapting to different demands as the years rolled by. In the process Caldecott has had to make a difficult transition from 'country school for working men's children' to therapeutic community, the change to an extent forced upon it by the increasingly vulnerable youngsters it has come to shelter.

A scrutiny of the those admitted to Caldecott at different times since its foundation illustrates some of these trends. Not all of the entrants are as needy as Siobhan and the perceptions of children's problems have also altered over time. Both these trends are manifest in the style of the intervention offered to children and in other aspects of the resident population, such as children's length of stay and destinations after leaving. To provide some picture of the changes in the characteristics of children admitted to the Caldecott Community over the years, we have analysed the backgrounds, presenting problems and destinations of 300 children leaving Caldecott between 1911 and 1990. This represents a one in four random sample of all leavers on whom information was available in the Community archives. It also includes the children in the follow-up study, described later on, namely all residents who left the Community between 1986 and 1990. This overview gives us an indication of changes in Community membership.

Prior to the Second World War, most referrals came directly from parents or relatives, or from charities and other sponsors of needy children. As might be expected, links with London were and remain particularly strong. An important source of referrals was the child guidance unit at the Tavistock clinic set up in the 1920s. Great Ormond Street Hospital, the London Jewish Hospital in the East End, the Invalid Children's Association as well as individual doctors, probation officers and psychologists have also extensively used the Community.

Other referrals have been the product of historical circumstance. Refugees sent by the British German Association continued to arrive during and after World War II. Leila Rendel's close friendship with Kurt Hahn, Lola Hahn Warburg and Henrietta Szold, all of whom did so much for those displaced by the conflict, explains this particular occurrence. Another unusual example, this time of individual sponsorship, is of a police officer who recommended Caldecott for a youngster accused of stealing a Union Jack worth four pounds from the local scout hut. The policeman's initiative and persistence persuaded the court and he also raised the money for the fees. The archives at Caldecott abound not only with examples of the munificence of the rich but also the enthusiasm and devotion of those far less well off.

During the first three decades, most children were the offspring of 'honest people who could not cope' such as widows, divorcees, lone fathers or deserted mothers. Some were nominated by local worthies, such as clergy, while others were born, occasionally out of wedlock, to the domestic staff of nobility. Titled ladies saw the welfare of such children as part of their supervising role, although, as Roy Parker has suggested, there was often an economic motive in their interest in that they did not want servants with dependent children. Other parents applied directly: we found a letter from a lone father seeking a place for his son who was to be supported by the railway trade union, the NUR.

So, as the following graph illustrates, in the first decade of its existence, the Community took nearly all its referrals from parents or voluntary organisations or from a combination of the two. It was concerned with the 'deserving poor' and in meeting an identified gap in provision, namely for children who were neither destitute and dependent on poor law institutions nor more affluent and therefore able to find shelter in boarding schools. The needs of this 'middle group' of children slowly became recognised in much special education provision and in the growth

Graph 1: Source of referrals to the Caldecott Community 1911-1990

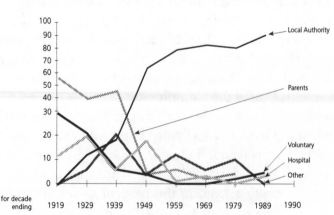

A Life Without Problems?

of the state boarding schools during the 1930s; needs which, as the graph shows, have become increasingly taken up by local authorities.

The children admitted in the early years had to be honest and deserving but, most important, they had to be clever. They were seen as unfortunate and, because of their family situation, unable to fulfil their considerable potential. This element of selection however did not entirely exclude difficult children and there were often hints of problems, for example in those described as 'naughty', 'disobedient' or 'soiling'. However, there were very few delinquents in the early years. The worst case we came across was a boy committed to care for stealing four penknives. He was the responsibility of the local probation department who, nevertheless, were anxious to secure a benign, caring placement for him; a task which required a considerable and presumably voluntary effort on their part to raise the fees.

Leila Rendel felt her Community was less suited to delinquent boys than institutions such as those run by George Lyward and others. It was with singular reluctance that she briefly accepted the recognition of the Community as a junior approved school during the war years. The admission of young delinquents was part of a bargain struck with the Home Office for financial support and accommodation. This pattern endures to this day. While other specialist centres have moved towards the older disturbed adolescent – the villains of the modern era – Caldecott has stuck with the younger victims.

The emphasis in those pre-war days was very much on those children who would benefit from a boarding school environment. But Caldecott stood out as something different. It was not part of the childcare system in which local authorities and voluntary organisations were providing cottage homes, neither was it part of the sector of small private boarding schools that aped the muscular Christianity of the more prestigious preparatory and public schools. Caldecott from the start was special in its intake and style. It best fitted into the 'progressive school' movement whose history has been charted by Maurice Bridgeland in *Pioneer Work with Maladjusted Children,* although it never achieved the size and stability and middle-class role of Bedales or the Quaker schools.

It was also, effectively a school for girls. As the following graph illustrates, in the first decade of its existence there were nine girls at Caldecott for every boy. This pattern has reversed over the years so that of the 60

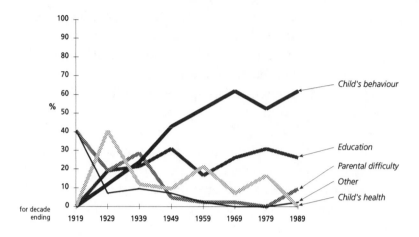

children who left the Community between 1986 and 1990, three-quarters were boys. Those referred to Caldecott have also got older over the years. All of Miss Leila's first group of entrants were aged eight years or less but today less than a third are below that age. But other patterns have endured. The mean length of stay has remained much the same throughout the 80 years of Caldecott's existence, about four years. The founding mothers kept them a bit longer, just a year or so more.

What reasons were given by the referrer for placing a child at the Community? Difficult behaviour as a primary reason has only pre-dominated since the 1940s. Before then, a child was most likely to be sent to Caldecott for health reasons or because their parents could not cope. Indeed, 'delicate' health, so much a concern in the early years of Caldecott's development – and sadly underestimated today – lasted long into the 1970s as a presenting factor in referrals. Now it is the child's behaviour that local authorities prioritise as their reason for seeking a place. But beneath the changing bureaucratic terminology, the needs of the children have remained much the same over the last eight decades.

The rate of referrals to the Community has fluctuated over the years but the nature of the task has meant that the difficulties of making ends meet and achieving a balance of residents which would sustain a healthy Community have remained constant. In the early days referrals were frequent, well in excess of what the Community could absorb. But it was still a struggle.

Graph 3: Proportion of boys and girls entering Caldecott, 1911-1990

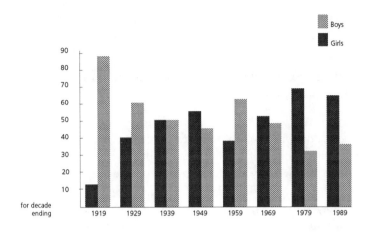

The difficulties and the qualities of the Community are captured in a letter of 1934 from Mr Garry Stagg. When returning the application form, he wrote a hand written letter to Leila Rendel which said:

> I enclose this duly filled up with the exception of one item – that of parents' income. This last point is difficult as I have now given up teaching (where naturally I had a fixed salary) and have taken an old house in Derbyshire to run as a guest house. Thus I can say all too truthfully that I have no income at all and doubt very much whether any profit will be shown until we have been established for at least three years. Peter's fees will have to be paid, like all my other bills, out of the overdraft allowed me by the bank.

Caldecott were cautious about Mr Stagg's motives but sympathetic because of Peter's pressing needs. Needless to say the fees were duly reduced. Such personal favours from Leila Rendel were not uncommon and, although she liked to appear completely in charge of such decisions, her philosophy was clear – to meet the child's needs first and let the finance sort itself out. However, there were occasional examples of primness and moral censoriousness in dealing with applications. For example, in a letter to a prospective parent in May 1919, Leila Rendel wrote, 'we do not object to taking illegitimate children although we are primarily a working-mens' children's boarding school'. The applicant was encouraged to look elsewhere.

The early referrers were mainly parents and schools. This was Caldecott's 'market' and it helped shape the type of care on offer. Parents with young children desired a caring environment but others required discipline and were attracted by the innovative methods attempted in the early years of the Community. For example, even as early as 1919, the Community wrote to a prospective parent, hesitant at the regimented nature of so many other boarding schools,

> In answer to your letter received this morning although we have never taken a definite stand with regard to the militarist question certainly the tendency of our whole teaching and upbringing is non military. The children have Swedish exercises daily and we have recently started a lodge of the Woodcraft Chivalry which as you probably know hopes to supply the need for some sort of Scout work upon non-military lines. Our children are taught from the earliest the elementary responsibility of citizenship and there is a large amount of self-government in the Community.

Many of these values endure today, even for those children whose parents are only dimly aware of Caldecott's existence. This approach was clearly attractive to parents numbed by the horrors of the Great War.

Exceptional placements were also made. Some children aged two, three and four were offered to the nursery and they stayed for longer than the norm, some for as long as 12 years. Caldecott became a long-term alternative to the family and coped with dislocations of all sorts, many of which like mental illness, divorce and alcoholism were implicit rather than explicit in the papers we scrutinised.

Thankfully, some demands on the Community have been extinguished. Before 1939 grave fears of infectious disease influenced decisions about accepting referrals and searching questions were always asked about illness in the child and family. TB families in particular were approached with extreme caution. Many of those taken in needed to live out of London because of allergies, asthma or illnesses exacerbated by over-crowding and poverty. For one child in the 1930s, the alternative to Caldecott was the Margate Sea Bathing Hospital, presumably a placement that nowadays would be seen as posing more a health risk than a cure. How easily we forget that, until relatively recently, the health needs of children were particularly pressing. This demand for boarding has largely disappeared.

We have already identified the Second World War as a watershed for Caldecott. It produced new categories of needy children and a rapid increase in lone parents. There was a temporary influx of Jewish refugees but Caldecott itself was also on the move making life difficult. For example, one parent, a foreign national, had to get a permit to visit the East Kent area because of War restrictions prior to D-Day. The shortages of wartime made it hard to clothe the children adequately or to arrange for regular family contacts. Some children's problems were also exacerbated by the changes in family structures brought about by the war, not least father's return after a long absence. Children found it difficult to fit back into their families and long-term plans for reunion often had to be revised.

Yet the children seemed to present few behaviour problems in these early years and were mostly able, promising children in unfortunate and limiting situations. There is little evidence in the records or from the early graduates who still visit the Community of serious behaviour difficulties. Perhaps comparisons are unfair. We know so much more about the current residents. Prior to 1945 the records are slight and reviews of children's progress were the exception rather than the rule. Neither were external consultants much employed to justify the placement of a child at the Community. Most decisions were made by the founding mothers and they remained unchallenged, indeed, in many cases uncommunicated. It must be remembered, of course, that typewriters were cumbersome and long-distance communication was slow and difficult. The Community only had one telephone until 1971. Thus widespread consultation was difficult. Telegrams were used a great deal and in one case where a girl from the Community was admitted to Great Ormond Street, daily telegrams were sent from the hospital to the Community informing Leila of her condition. Sadly, the girl died.

As local authorities and professionals took a greater hand in referrals to the Community after 1945, so the correspondence with parents - often about very mundane issues such as clothing, especially that left behind in other institutions - becomes less frequent. The question of contributions to fees disappears. In the 1930s, parents were expected to find one pound a week, by the 1940s this had risen to 25 shillings. By contemporary standards this represents a lot of money for hard up parents, about a third of an average salary. But in real terms the fees have risen enormously to about five and a half times a general wage in 1992. Only local authorities can afford the level of professionalism now on offer at the Community.

The records give us our first glimpse of the future prospects of children leaving the Community. Many went on to college and to successful careers, some in the major professions. Again sponsorship was key. Leila helped her children by writing direct to Admirals and Major-Generals to get children into the armed forces and in 1927 wrote direct to the chairman of the London North East Railway literally demanding a job for a boy interested in trains. In 1946 she was in personal communication with the apprentice master at Heals in Tottenham Court Road to help a girl take a job as a shop assistant. Well connected and motivated entirely by the needs of the child, Leila Rendel haunted the upper classes with requests. Many were approached for work on estate farms and in stables including Leonard and Dorothy Elmhirst at Dartington who in 1926 were asked to find agricultural employment for a 14 year old boy. This letter was simply addressed to Leonard Elmhirst, Totnes. Movingly, there is still a letter in the file from this boy dated 1980 saying that he had just retired after a long and happy working life and expressing his gratitude to Caldecott for its help.

As the following table shows, although the intake to the Community has become more difficult over time, an increasing proportion of leavers has gone back to live with relatives or set up their own home. Early on, many children were withdrawn early by their parents, usually because of improved family situations. Others went on to other boarding schools, either because of their bad performance at Caldecott or to fulfil their academic abilities, but on the whole very few children were expelled from the Community.

Once again, some outcomes are specific to an historical context. In the early years, some children died at Caldecott, thankfully an outcome that would be very unusual today. One or two of the approved school boys sheltered during the war moved directly to prison, again something which has not happened since. Miss Leila's eye to the Armed Services as an employer is evident in the number of leavers to the forces, a pattern which endured into the 1970s but which today is more difficult.

With increased interest by the State, referral patterns have become less varied and the procedures for entry to the Community more pre-

Graph 4: Destination of leavers from Caldecott, 1911-1990

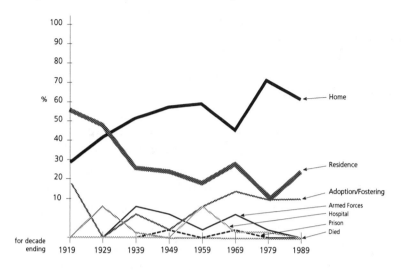

dictable. Children now come almost exclusively from local education authorities and social services departments. Applications include the perspectives of several professionals and have elaborate assessments of children's needs. Clearly present day candidates are far more difficult and damaged than were their predecessors and today's entrants are of very mixed abilities.

All residents are now of compulsory school age and, of course, since the early 1980s, abuse, whether sexual, physical or emotional, has become a major feature of their backgrounds. Only one case of physical beating by a father was found in the records prior to 1960 and sexual abuse was never mentioned, either as a family feature or even as a possibility in the background assessments made by psychiatrists and psychologists. It seems highly likely, therefore, that evidence of abuse over the years will have been missed.

Conclusions

This historical survey of young people admitted to the Caldecott Community confirms many of the points made in the previous sections. A watershed in the type and nature of referrals took place after the Second World War and, with the subsequent introduction of enlightened children's legislation and the increasing power of professional groups, prompted, belatedly perhaps, a re-think of Caldecott's approach and

---

management. While present patterns of referral were well established by 1945, the wider context has changed markedly. The situations that would lead a local authority to place a six year old in a residential school are quite different now from those of even 20 years ago, particularly as repeated failures in alternative family placement are now a common reason. But, generally, since the War we have found relative consistency in referrals.

As we shall see, the backgrounds of young people in the Community today are far more turbulent and riddled with complex problems than was the case in the early years. This has had two effects. Not only are individual children more difficult to help but the resident population at Caldecott has also become more disturbed as a whole. Opportunities to soften the impact of a troublesome child in a sea of normality are much reduced. Interestingly, this danger haunted the founding mothers who struggled long to maintain a 'healthy mix' of children and consistently rejected the designation of special school. Such independence was bought dearly in cash terms as the Caldecott Community defied bureaucratic classification and cut itself off from much statutory support.

But Caldecott has survived. As we shall see, in the last 20 years, across England and Wales, the number of children in local authority care living in residential settings has fallen from 37,000 to 8,000. More vulnerable children now stay at home, hopefully with local community support. Reductions in the populations in residential EBD schools are less marked but the trend is still one of decline with the current population hovering at around 10,000. As the two sectors now cater for roughly equal numbers of children, the special boarding school has become a major provider of residential care for separated children. How long this situation will endure is difficult to guess but given the decline in overall numbers, it seems highly likely that the children placed in residential care will include very difficult and unstable cases and, clearly, Caldecott will be one of the destinations chosen.

This historical evidence shows Caldecott's adaptability and ability to evolve, qualities which have facilitated the Community's success. Foreseeing and responding to changing conceptions of need has helped the Community's maintain its market during times when attitudes towards residential care have been decidedly chilly.

"

Siobhan's referral to Caldecott

In her 'life story', Siobhan recounts how she came into care with her youngest brother Nigel. Relationships with her mother had become intolerable and the local children's home was seen as providing temporary respite. But Siobhan's behaviour did not improve and, to make matters worse, she was separated from Nigel who was admitted to hospital suffering from anaemia. Sheila, the children's social worker, became convinced that return was highly unlikely in the near future and that Nigel and Siobhan had different needs. Apart from her appalling behaviour, there was the possibility that Siobhan had been sexually abused. All this took place in February 1990.

A decision was made to separate the children and, on his return from hospital, Nigel moved to a foster placement. This only served to infuriate Siobhan more. She refused to go to school or to have anything to do with a place called Caldecott which Sheila suggested she might enjoy. Would she like to visit? No, she would not.

Undeterred, Sheila wrote to the Community in March describing Siobhan's circumstances and, as she was of the right age and clearly amenable to treatment, they requested more details. Sheila went to look for herself a few weeks later and this prompted the Caldecott referral panel to consider which of the living groups Siobhan would best fit. Hornbeam, with three vacancies for girls, seemed the most likely and care workers were asked to visit Siobhan. At the same time, the precaution was taken of having one of the consultants glance at the referral papers.

Having worked closely in each of the parts that make up the Caldecott Community, and having carefully monitored their fluctuations in mood, we have come to the conclusion that one of the best indicators of a healthy unit is that all the beds are occupied. Hornbeam had vacancies because staff were preoccupied with the difficulties caused by three boys. They could have taken Siobhan at any time but the opportunity to visit and make an assessment never arose. In Woodside, by contrast, the imminent planned departure of an adolescent girl prompted them to seek a replacement. So it was in May that Siobhan was to meet Kate Edwards, who was to play a very significant role in her life.

I was sitting in this children's home in Bromley and I was well pissed off. Nigel had gone and moved onto another children's home. I didn't even know where he was. And I saw my mum every week but I had nothing to say to her. And there was no school. And there was this place Caldecott but nothing seemed to be happening. So I was expecting this woman called Pat from Hornbeam and this lady walks in. I said 'Oh, you must be Pat from Hornbeam then?' and she said 'No, I'm Kate from Woodside'. 'Oh, so you're not Pat from Hornbeam'. 'No, Kate from Woodside, that's me'. And we had a laugh. That's how I know Kate and that's how I got to Woodside.

Many years ago, a decision to accept a child would be swiftly followed by the placement. In today's professional world everything takes a little longer. Include the extensive questions that the finance officers raise and the whole process can be very lengthy. It was the middle of June before the local education authority could approve Caldecott's plans for Siobhan's schooling and the case conference to review Sheila's decision to place Siobhan at Caldecott did not take place until the end of the month. Financial arrangements – great sheaves of papers which dwarf the professional reports – were not complete until mid-July.

Unfortunately, none of these timescales made much sense to Siobhan who, despite the careful explanations by her social worker, Sheila, and the full description of Woodside by Kate Edwards grew increasingly anxious. This took its toll on her health and in the last weeks of July – four months after she first heard of Caldecott – Siobhan developed Bell's Palsy.

Woodside kept a place open for her and a final date for her arrival was set for the 23rd of August. Even then, plans nearly faltered at the last minute.

> *What happened?*
> S. I ran away on the morning I was supposed to go.
> *You didn't want to go to Caldecott?*
> S. No, it wasn't Caldecott, I didn't want to go anywhere. I didn't want to do anything. I didn't even know where I was going or what would happen if I didn't go. I was just being a little bugger. I was good at that.
> *And so what happened?*

S. Well, I just came back to Bromley. I had nowhere to go, so I came back. And then Kate came to pick me up. At that point I didn't know where I was or where I was going, so I just went along. Kate was good to me. She didn't try to make me do too much. I just went along and it was OK.

We saw in previous sections how the period since 1945 has been marked by an increasing professionalisation both in the agencies sending children to Caldecott and in the Community itself. But the child's view of the world has not changed in this time. Now, as before, they see this place 'Caldecott' quite differently from the adults. They receive information about their new home or next placement with a sense of foreboding. Like Siobhan, they are far more caught up in their current difficulties - of leaving home, of losing her brother Nigel, of being away from school, of not knowing what the future holds - than they are with the promises of a therapeutic community. While the professionals check and check again, the children sit and wait, captured by the next episode of *Neighbours* or some other immediate event in their own lives.

Patterns of referral

As we shall see, many of the decisions taken on Siobhan's behalf during the summer months of 1990 will have long-term consequences for her life. Sheila's decision to consider Caldecott in the first place, Hornbeam's decision to pass the referral on to the more stable Woodside and Kate's spontaneous rapport with Siobhan; in time these will all be seen as important to Siobhan's good progress. On the other side of this coin, the decisions made at Caldecott and within the referral agencies are fundamental to the Community's survival. To use economic parlance, the marginal costs of providing residence are low and operating with just ten empty beds can be enough to bring a centre to a halt as income falls for the same expenditure. Many therapeutic communities have faltered because of these conditions in recent years.

At any one time, the Community is dealing with about 25 children who have been referred for each of the 80 beds. However, less than a third of referrals eventually arrive. A glance at the numbers under consideration at any moment gives a good indication of the Community's economic fortunes. The next graph illustrates how financial constraints upon local authorities depressed referrals to Caldecott in the early 1990s. The immediate impact of the *Children Act*, 1989, implemented in the autumn of 1991, which temporarily reduced the number of children looked after, may also have had an effect on the figures.

Graph 5: The number of referrals being processed by the Community 1990-1993

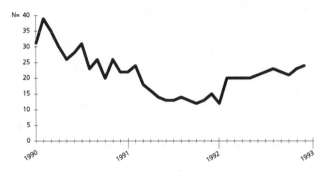

Despite these fluctuations in referral, the Community has managed to maintain a reasonable occupancy rate in recent years. The following graph shows the proportion of beds that were slept in over the first two years of the research. It also contrasts the situation in three of the eight living units within Caldecott. Woodside was consistently full throughout this period, numbers in Mayfield varied whereas in Lacton Hall – which admitted adolescents from other parts of the Community – there were more vacancies than residents at the end of our scrutiny.

Graph 6: Occupancy rates at the Caldecott Community and within three selected units during the first two years of study

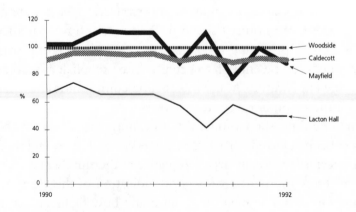

What do these data reveal? Initially, they show that within a large residential centre, there are several sub-units which may have quite contrasting fortunes. This makes the management of referrals extremely difficult. Only Woodside had all of its beds occupied during these two years, carefully timing the arrival of new residents to coincide with the departure of the old. At Mayfield, there were periods when the placement of new arrivals was made difficult by either the behaviour of other residents or by staff shortages - two factors that very often are linked. At Lacton Hall, the loss of staff and an increased anxiety about the young people's situations reached almost crisis proportions so that at the beginning of 1992 this one unit accounted for five of the eight vacancies in the entire Community.

A large residential centre can balance its strong units against its weaker parts. If Lacton Hall had been an independent home, it would have closed. Sheltered under the protective wing of the Community, it has recovered. However, the difference between success and failure for those managing Caldecott is small. It would take only three or four of the living units to suffer as did the adolescent centre for the entire Community to come under threat.

No simple system will ensure that all vacancies are swiftly filled, especially in a co-educational centre. Children share bedrooms at Caldecott and the organisation of some units means that equal numbers of boys and girls are needed. When we looked at all referrals to Caldecott in 1990, 128 children in the year, we found that three-quarters were boys. However, over two-fifths of girls considered for a place at the Community were accepted compared with less than a third (29%) of boys.

Table 1: Numbers of boys and girls referred and admitted to the Community in 1990

	Boys	Girls	Total
Admitted	28	14	42
Not admitted	68	18	86
Total	96	32	128

These findings would suggest that, although girls referred to Caldecott tend to be more difficult than the boys, this is balanced by the Community's threshold for entry being lower for girls. It is all part of making

Caldecott work, a task which requires flexibility on the part of its managers and those in local authorities.

The processes involved in choosing a placement for a child will obviously vary between child-care professionals but they are usually protracted. The first step when presented with a very difficult child is usually to find all the available options. We were interested in how individual social workers learn of Caldecott. Most have the Community recommended to them by other professionals, especially from child guidance, the Maudsley Hospital and the Tavistock Clinic. Social workers also frequently mention regional resource centres, advertisements in journals and 'word of mouth' as the source. This would suggest that the reputation of Caldecott and other therapeutic communities is very important in the initial stages of any referral.

The delay between initial referral and a decision being made about whether a place will be offered to a child is evident from a scrutiny of the 128 referrals just described. Even for the three-quarters who did not arrive at Caldecott, two and a half months elapsed on average between the first telephone call and the application being withdrawn. In one exceptional case, over a year of negotiations between professionals went by before it was accepted that the child did not have the mental capacity to play a full role in the Community. For those children who do find a place, an additional month is needed and the longest period between referral and arrival was the seven months taken by Siobhan.

Most referrals were withdrawn after a careful dialogue between Caldecott and the local authority. In about a fifth of cases, the Community refused to take a child even though social services or education representatives were sure that they had found the appropriate placement. The commonest reason given was that the child was too old or too aggressive. Some referrals simply could not cope with the educational demands of Caldecott and occasionally a disability, such as epilepsy, led to a refusal. In two cases, the child was entirely acceptable to Community staff but they had no bed to offer when the local authority needed it.

In another 12% of referrals, the local authority withdrew its application despite Caldecott's belief that it had something to give to the child. Frequently, objections stemmed from the views of education representatives within the agency or from finance officers who balked at the cost. Although by most standards the charges are not excessive, they are subjected to rigorous scrutiny when long-term placements are being considered. Finally, the distance from the child's home and the poor facilities offered to parents at Caldecott have deterred a few social workers, mindful of their responsibility under the *Children Act, 1989* to maintain the child's contact with relatives.

We came to understand the referral process as a series of hurdles which needed to be cleared before the placement was agreed. These jumps include: scrutiny by the Caldecott referral panel; the local authority representative visiting the Community; a residential social worker visiting the child; an admission conference and a financial agreement. Less frequently, the process might also involve the child visiting Caldecott or one of the Community's specialists looking at the papers. The majority of referrals fall at the first hurdle and, while the decision is not swift, it is usually conclusive. For ten children, however, negotiations were lengthy and several obstacles were overcome but the child was still placed elsewhere and in three cases an arrival date had been agreed before the local authority withdrew its application at the last minute.

We decided to look much more closely at the 14 children referred during 1990 who went through the full selection procedure but either a place offered was not accepted or the application was ultimately unsuccessful. The children had many features similar to those admitted to Caldecott but there were key differences.

The family situation of both groups was characterised by high levels of neglect and maltreatment, as well as relatively high rates of mental illness and financial problems. But for those who found a place at Caldecott, stress factors tended to be multiple so, for example, illness was frequently compounded by homelessness, parents' criminality, alcohol misuse and even drug abuse.

The comparison also revealed important differences which may affect the choices made by social workers and other professionals at the point of referral. The unsuccessful candidates displayed less severe stress in certain crucial areas, particularly abuse. It may be that the need to protect the child was less pressing and, with extra time, social workers and education officials had more options open to them including the choice of several placements. While foster care may have been appropriate for children like Siobhan, there were rarely families available for the older victim of maltreatment.

We have highlighted distance from home as being a factor in the late withdrawal of some children, but there was little difference in the geographical distribution of those accepted and those rejected for a place in the Community. As has been the case since the 1930s, most referrals came from the South and South-east of England. One of the 14 children who came close to being admitted to Caldecott in 1990 came from the South-west, another from Wales and a third from Yorkshire. Only in discussions about this last case were concerns raised about the distance between Caldecott and home.

Although it is lengthy, social workers and other professionals do not seem to object to the referral process. Those involved with these 14 children had more right to feel aggrieved than most, having almost reached the finishing line, but only two felt strongly about the matter. One commented that, while it was thorough, discussions were largely paper-based exercises; she was surprised the child was not formally assessed. This child was subsequently accepted at a smaller therapeutic community which had provision similar to Caldecott. The other social worker, in contrast, thought the referral process among the best she had encountered.

So why did the referral process collapse at the last hurdle for these 14 children? In four cases the child's disruptive behaviour clearly played a part as weary residential social workers expressed unease. In other cases, rejection came not from psychology or behaviour but from the child's age. Nowadays Caldecott readily takes children under the age of 13 but in 1990 there was a 'bulge' in the senior age group, especially among boys. To rectify this imbalance the upper age limit for boys was temporarily lowered to 10. Although some of the children turned away would have benefited from the work of the Community, the effect of introducing more boys might have proved detrimental to other residents, not least the established groups of girls. Thus, the referral process took account not only of the candidate's needs but also those already resident, a feature not always apparent in other residential settings.

In many cases Caldecott was competing for the child's placement. The psychologist's reports on four of the 14, for example, recommended only that the child be placed in a therapeutic setting. The Community was frequently judged against the strengths and weaknesses of the child's placement at the time of referral, especially for social workers anxious not to disrupt the life of the child more than was necessary.

We can see this in the case of a nine year old boy whose social worker was given six months by the High Court to find a permanent placement. The boy had become a Ward of Court. His mother, a manic depressive, had been in and out of psychiatric hospitals and his grandparents were concerned about the effect this was having on the boy's behaviour. Reports described him as 'a really mixed up kid'. He had been placed in long-term foster care but, due to his aggressive behaviour and temper tantrums, placements continually broke down and he was placed in a small residential unit as a 'stop-gap' while a major review was undertaken. It was then that the Court requested a permanent placement.

After attempts to find a foster home through the national press had failed, social workers turned to Caldecott and the referral process began. Due to the degree of difficulty posed by the boy and the high level of external scrutiny, this was protracted. During this time the boy settled in his 'stop-gap' placement and his difficult behaviour subsided. In the end, the judge agreed with professionals that, given his unsettled past, it was more beneficial for him to remain at his current placement than to move elsewhere. Just as Caldecott assesses the children thoroughly, so social workers assess the child's individual needs. It is only when the two are in agreement that a place at the Community is offered and accepted.

The reasons given for finding an alternative placement were, therefore, specific to each child's circumstance. Two brothers, for example, were referred to the Community together as it was decided they should not be parted. Caldecott did everything they could to accommodate the boys, but, since one was over 10 years old, they both went elsewhere. Again, it was the least disruptive option that was chosen.

If other options are available, where did these 14 children eventually go? Eight went to other long-term residential settings, mostly special boarding schools but two went to other therapeutic communities. Two others remained in the short-term residential placements where they had been waiting while alternatives such as Caldecott were considered. One boy remained at home and three went to special foster homes.

In the long-term, did these children who nearly found a niche within the Community fare well in the alternatives found for them? The answer is generally no. As we shall see, Caldecott is not entirely successful with troubled children but it does provide stability for most who stay within its walls. Only two of those going to other settings avoided the unsettling experience of a placement breakdown and only two received some form of professional treatment for their problems. Eventually, most of these 14 rejected referrals, like those accepted for placement, return to live with relatives but those coming to Caldecott do at least have the promise of some prolonged respite and some insight into their problems.

In conclusion, the unsuccessful candidates usually had more options available to them than the general population of Caldecott children. Their family backgrounds were less difficult and they presented fewer acute or potentially dangerous problems. Over the years, Caldecott has increasingly admitted children requiring 52 week care. Many of these children are at risk of abuse from family members and return for long periods during school holidays is not always possible. This feature was far less marked among the unsuccessful referrals. Many went on to boarding schools which allowed the child to go home during school vacations. But, even so, they did not fare particularly well, thus providing our first indication of the possible worth of the Caldecott experience.

"

The group

Siobhan arrived at Woodside in August 1990. She was introduced to Mandy with whom she was to share a room. Woodside has none of the imposing grandeur of the main house. It is relatively homely and Siobhan settled quickly, at least to the extent that she was well behaved and placid. This was not the first time that Siobhan had moved to strange surroundings. She knew how to hide her nerves, present as confident and worldly-wise and to enjoy the attention that greets the arrival of a new child.

In previous homes, Siobhan had learnt of the circumstances of other children from the grapevine of gossip and half-truths which grow in any large group setting. In a therapeutic community, the passing of information is frequent and, potentially at least, more above board. Every week, the group, which is the children and staff of Woodside, have a meeting. (This way of operating is broadly similar across the Community). At this gathering many issues are discussed and when a new person arrives it is used as an opportunity for everybody to introduce themselves.

It can take many years before we begin to get an insight into the lives of people with whom we work or share accommodation. At Caldecott, these barriers are swept aside and everything is more direct. What follows is a description of the first group meeting Siobhan attended. It is as she remembered it so there may be some inaccuracies. We will then give a little more detail on each of the children for we will come back to them and trace their progress as the study progresses. First, the meeting.

The meeting

I arrived on the Thursday and the meeting must have been on the Wednesday because they are every Wednesday. All of the group was there including two or three adults. Kate made us sit down and then she introduced me and asked everybody else to introduce themselves. I can't remember exactly what they all said but it was something like this.

Billy and Brian are brothers. They were two big fat boys. Billy said he was here because he was unhappy at home. Brian didn't say anything.

Tina said she was 13 and had been in Woodside for two years. She said she was at Caldecott because she had been sexually abused by her parents.

Tony and Thomas are black. Tony said his father was African and he had come to Caldecott because his dad had beat him and his brother very badly.

Keith was a bit odd. He didn't say very much at all.

Kevin is eleven and his brother was also at Caldecott. He was really cocky and went on for ages about how long he had been at Caldecott and how he shouldn't be here really but he couldn't keep his temper. I quite liked him really. He seemed quite nice.

Then there was Mandy who was also black and had also been sexually abused. I was quite shocked when she said it because we were sharing a room and when Tina said it I thought it was because she was making it up.

Then last of all there is Hayley who was really thin and lanky and I was really amazed when she said she was 16 and going to leave Woodside in the next few months. She wasn't very clever and everybody giggled when she spoke. I felt sorry for her really.

When it was my turn I just said I was Siobhan and I had come here because I didn't get on with my mum. I told them about my brother Nigel and how I missed him and hoped he would come here as well.

The other children

Billy and Brian Adams

These boys came from an intact family, one of the few in the study where the children shared biological parents and both parents still lived together in the family home. In addition to the two boys, then aged 15 and 13, there was a four year old sister. Father appeared to have enjoyed little influence in the family, being very passive and refusing to be drawn into any of our interviews. The files indicated that he disappeared from time to time, possibly to prison, and this caused disruption in the family and anxiety in the boys. Mum was named Beatrice, but preferred to be called Beatie. She grew up in children's homes and is a large, ebullient, articulate and chaotic person, well practised in manipulating any social and welfare services that will listen to her. All the family, except the father, were obese. They lived in a potentially pleasant three bedroom council flat in a low rise estate in SW London. However, the home was damp and, when all the family members were present, overcrowded. Beatie's life was dominated by a series of campaigns, one was for a larger council flat; another was to obtain a place for the 'baby' Sarah at a nursery school.

The boys, Billy and Brian, were placed at Caldecott as a result of serious developmental, behavioural and learning difficulties which their local school found impossible to deal with and which involved constant clashes between teachers and Beatie. Their mother in her words 'couldn't cope with them – I was having a nervous breakdown'. The boys had a period of three or four months away from home in a therapeutic community during which time they attended a small local school and did well. However, on their return home the situation deteriorated again. At the same time father returned from one of his absences and there were clashes between him and Billy, at that time about ten years old. It was decided that the boys would be better away from home and Caldecott was suggested by the educational psychologist as a place which might be able to meet the boys' needs, especially Billy's. As Beatie did not want the boys to be separated, Brian was admitted to the junior section at Caldecott. The two children went home every other weekend and the mother and father visited Caldecott in between. During these visits, father usually stayed outside in the car, apparently so as to avoid arguments with Billy.

Tina Richmond

Tina, 13, had been at Caldecott for two years. She and her sister had been sexually abused by both her mother and father. Her mother was viewed as highly dangerous, having assaulted Tina on a visit 12 months previously. On the occasions we met her, Mrs Richmond gave no indication of her part in her daughter's abuse. We knew that in 1986 her children, then six and seven years old, told a neighbour of their maltreatment and were removed under emergency provisions. In the following four years they frequently moved between foster homes and residential care. During this time their mother was denied contact. Mrs Richmond claimed to have no knowledge of the abuse and felt that she had been treated badly by the professionals. Tina was judged to have been the mostly seriously abused child in the family and as she manifested more behavioural disturbance than her sister, who was fostered near to her mother's house. Tina had been resident for two years when Siobhan arrived.

Tony and Thomas Bozzi

Tony and his brother Thomas are the sons of an African father and a Caribbean mother. When we started studying Caldecott they were eight and 10 years old having been in Woodside for two years. As babies, the boys were deserted by their father and were fostered. Their mother used to visit them every six weeks. Later she asked for day care funding for them but they showed signs of difficult behaviour from an early age, causing trouble at school, kicking, biting and other signs of disturbance. When they were four and six, Tony and Thomas were sent to their father's family in Africa for 18 months. During this time Thomas was severely beaten by his father – he still has the scars. On return, they went through four children's homes before being placed in Woodside. Since their arrival, Tony's behaviour had improved slightly and Thomas had blossomed.

Keith Taylor

Keith is the middle of three children of a single mother, all with different fathers. His mother had lived with five different partners; the only one Keith formed an attachment to was unfortunately killed in a road accident. The boy was frenzied with grief. His mother, Liz, found his behaviour problematic even as a toddler and at six he was having violent rages both at home and at school. Liz could not cope and Keith was fostered several times. His disturbed behaviour was linked with severe panic attacks, during which he would physically assault those around him and it became impossible for him to function in a normal school setting. It also led to more confrontations with his emotionally labile mother, who was at the point of breakdown when he was given a place as a weekly boarder at Caldecott.

Kevin Clarke

Kevin Clarke was eleven years old and his younger brother Neil – also at Caldecott – eight on admission to Caldecott. Like Siobhan they had experienced rejection by their father and several aborted attempts to join their family in Ireland. They too have a history of physical but not sexual abuse by their father and at least one of the partners of their mother. The boys were placed in Caldecott because of severe behavioural difficulties at school. Kevin the older boy was particularly disturbed, having outbursts of violence. His teachers had noted bruises on his body, which he denied had been inflicted by anyone. Neil appeared to be less disturbed, was quieter, more 'normal' and easier to manage.

Mandy Atkinson

Mandy is Siobhan's age. She is black. Her mother is of Afro-Caribbean descent, her father is white from the East End of London. Mandy came to Woodside shortly before Siobhan and, in many respects, the two girls had similar histories and problems. However, as we shall see, they were to enjoy very different outcomes.

Hayley Clifton

Hayley had been at Caldecott for seven years by the time Siobhan arrived. She was badly neglected as a child but came to the Community for help with her education difficulties. She gained an enormous amount from the school's patient work but still presented as a rather inadequate but likeable young woman. Plans for Hayley's departure, probably to an independent living flat run by the Community in Ashford were being fashioned when Siobhan joined Woodside. Hayley's parents had become rather marginal to her life and were felt incapable of resuming care.

Conclusions

In this section we have our first glimpse of the children in Woodside, one of eight units that, together with the school, make up the Caldecott Community. We have viewed the circumstances of the residents from two angles; first from the information Siobhan collected at her first group meeting and then from our own researches with the children's families and their social workers. Quite clearly, each of the children is, in his or her own way, very vulnerable. But their vulnerability is manifest in different ways in different contexts. For the residential worker, abuse has a currency and families are seldom mentioned except as being responsible for that abuse. From the social worker's perspective – mindful that the child must move on from Caldecott – the family takes a greater salience. Both miss certain important features in the children's lives – their class, culture and race, for example and, while it is fundamental to the work of Caldecott, education does not take a high profile in professional descriptions of the children's situations.

So far in this study, we have introduced the idea of a gap existing between a professional view of the child's needs – increasingly apparent in Caldecott's work since the Second World War – and the perspective of the concerned lay person – evident in the strivings of Leila Rendel and the other founding mothers. Now a second strand, Caldecott as seen through the child's eyes, is becoming increasingly important in our deliberations. Let us bear these in mind as we move on to look more clinically at the circumstances and needs of the children whose progress we shall be following: that is, the 60 children who left the Community between 1986–1990.

The background characteristics of children at Caldecott

Most residential establishments shelter children with a variety of needs. Few, however, systematically audit their resident population and descriptions of the aims, objectives and purpose of residential centres frequently become lost in practice wisdom. The confusion that can occur was evident in the kinds of advice we were offered when we began this research. We were told that all the children had been sexually abused. As we shall see, whilst some have been sexually maltreated, most have not.

One member of staff, after reading previous Dartington research about the importance of contact between children absent in care and their families, commented, 'Oh, that's no use to us, the children don't have families.' Family relationships for Caldecott children are more strained than is common even for disadvantaged youngsters but the research revealed a more optimistic view than the observer had suggested.

Many outsiders have a similarly blinkered view of the Community. Some social workers see it as an anachronism; one said to us 'It's a lovely place but when I saw all those inner city kids, many of them black, roaming around a beautiful country house, I just felt what the hell are we doing?' So, as is often the case on entering residential centres, we were given a lot of opinions, some of which sought to justify Caldecott's approach, others which were critical but few which were based on evidence. Naturally, part of our task has been to take a sober look at the children, casting aside those emotions aroused by the plight of damaged and abused youngsters.

Is this dispassionate perspective relevant to work with troubled children? We think it is. Without knowing the needs of the children, the effectiveness of interventions cannot be judged. Unfortunately, few residential homes and schools know much about the characteristics of the children they look after. Recent reports on residential care, such as Pindown and Utting, have focused on children's rights and their immediate quality of life; evidence from places like Caldecott can help answer more fundamental questions, such as, who are these children? why are they like this? how does what is offered relate to their needs?

Our answers to these questions have been provided by a close look at all 60 children who left Caldecott between 1986 and 1990. We selected these dates in order to give us ample opportunity to see what happens to leavers during the three years after departure. We will review this evidence later. First we shall explore their lives prior to Caldecott, including the difficulties they experienced at home, at school and in other social relationships. We also consider the ways in which various support agencies have responded to these problems. For example, we looked at who referred the children to Caldecott, whether that be child guidance, education departments or social services. It has been our experience that by understanding features of what we call the child's 'care career', the child's pathology and the ways in which agencies intervene to ease problems, we can predict, with a reasonable degree accuracy, long term out-comes, at least in general terms.

Caldecott is predominately a service for boys, only a quarter of those leaving the Community between 1986 and 1990 were girls. The service has also largely been catering for the younger child. Although there was considerable variation in ages, a third of the 60 children had arrived at Caldecott before their eighth birthday and over two-thirds had not pro-gressed to secondary school. These figures have to be set alongside the fact that the great majority of entrants to residential care in England and Wales are adolescents.

The Community is largely serving local authorities in and around London and it was therefore unsurprising to discover that ten per cent of the intake comes from minority ethnic groups. Kent was responsible for the greatest number of referrals, but overall 19 local authorities placed children during the period of scrutiny. Reflecting the complexity of need presented by Caldecott children, both social services and education tended to have been involved in planning, sometimes funding places jointly. In about half of cases, other agencies, including child guidance, schools psychology services and specialist health workers had also been involved.

At the point of referral, local authorities were primarily interested in the special residential schooling offered by the Community for children with educational and behavioural difficulties. Many indicated that had their Caldecott application been unsuccessful, they would have sought a place in a boarding special school. Other residential settings, such as com-munity homes with or without education on the premises and provided by social services, had rarely been considered, although specialised fos-tering had been a serious possibility for one in ten of the 60 children we scrutinised.

Referral agencies sought a combination of special needs education and a caring environment which would include therapy and intensive personalised care and nurture for the child. They seemed unconcerned about Caldecott's geographical location and while one in six professionals looked to the Community because of its nearness to the child's home, as many again saw the distance from relatives as beneficial.

There is a danger in over-emphasising or misinterpreting the reason given by professionals for seeking a place at Caldecott. It is not insignificant that in over 90% of cases, knowledge of the Community and its work was important in professional decisions to refer a child. In short, there was a 'Caldecott' factor based on positive experiences in the past and the Community's good reputation. They may not know the facts of the situation but these people certainly 'know' Caldecott can provide a workable solution to the problems presented by the child for whom they are responsible.

A partial perspective can be gained from the concerns expressed by the referring authorities. Professionals were largely worried about the child's psychological health, disturbed behaviour and special educational needs. The benefits of permanence offered by the placement were also attractive. At least one of these concerns was mentioned in three-quarters of referral papers. Less common for some cases was the rejection of the child's family, experiences of abuse and violence which cropped up in about one-third of the application papers.

One way to summarise this evidence is to rank the factors according to the significance given to them in the local authority application. For each child, we ranked the three most important reasons for seeking a place at Caldecott. We then devised a score, using a method described in the following table, giving us one picture of how Caldecott is viewed by the world outside and also a perspective on the child's difficulties.

Table 2: Factors significant in the referral to Caldecott

	Score
Child's psychological health	130
Placement stability/permanency	60
Difficult/disturbed behaviour	49
Educational needs	48
Abusing families	12
Absence of immediate family	9
Rejecting family	9
Aggression or violence	8
Over-protective family	5
Persistent absconding	4
Delinquency	3
Child protection	3
Danger to self	3

Three factors selected and ranked 1, 2, 3. Score calculated by scoring 3 for first choice 2 for second and 1 for third choice. (N=60, Maximum score 360).

Children's family situations

Children have families. This is not always welcome news to residential centres which not only tire of the hassle of sharing parenting tasks with relatives who may live many miles away, but also mistrust them. After all, a great deal of psychological research has demonstrated how children can be harmed by poor early nurturing and most of those we are considering have enjoyed a less than satisfactory home life. Doubts about the viability of the family are frequently confirmed when children return home for visits or holidays. Nonetheless, most children looked after in residential care are closely attached to certain relatives, even if these family members live in generally unsatisfactory situations. Home is where most separated children want to be and, as we shall see, the natural family is the ultimate destination of most leavers.

Given their multiple difficulty, we might expect the families of children at Caldecott to be dislocated and to have experienced high levels of reconstitution. Household membership will be fluid, requiring residential staff continually to up-date information and assessments. We shall shortly discover whether Caldecott is able to overcome problems of distance and routine by keeping children in touch with home. It is now generally thought that contact with relatives, including siblings, grandparents and others is usually in the child's best interests and should be encouraged unless there are strong reasons to the contrary. This is even true of some adoption situations. Such a change in policy from the days of child rescue practised by Leila Rendel's contemporaries could not have been envisaged but given the short-comings of many child-care interventions, the natural family is likely to be the principal continuity in children's lives. After all, who will take over when Caldecott has completed its task?

Against this backdrop, it should cause few surprises to report that nearly nine in ten of the children had a place they regarded as home and close relatives living there. If Caldecott had been forced to close its doors during their stay, 79% of the children could have returned home. But having stressed the importance of the children's families, let us remember the many weaknesses of the home setting. All of these children were living at Caldecott because their relatives had ill-treated them or could not cope with the child's behaviour problems. Some had been injured by someone closely related to them. Most of the families had been severely disrupted, the number of cases where both mother and father still lived together was small (21%) and single-parenting (35%) was twice as common as step-parenting (14%).

The mere existence of a family home does not make it healthy or fulfilling. Sometimes a detailed research scrutiny seems superfluous. Even a glance at family circumstances reveals homes fraught with problems such as illness, abuse, addiction and poverty. Two-thirds of the children had experienced rejection, a third had been brought up in abusive environments and a quarter of the families were living in sub-standard accommodation. In a small number of cases the families could even be described as dangerous. The following table gives an indication of some of the stress factors playing on the households of Caldecott residents. While the level and range of difficulty are far higher than for the general population, only neglect and abuse applied to the majority of Caldecott children. It is the summation, sequence and interaction of stress factors that brings about harm.

Table 3: Stress factors in child's home at point of referral to the Community

	%		%
Neglect/abuse	70	Alcohol or drug abuse	19
Severe financial problems	35	Frequent membership change	12
Single-parent household	35	Criminality	19
Chronic unemployment	26	Homelessness	7
Poor housing	26	Physical illness	7
Mental illness	19	Physical handicap	2

We found that relationships in the children's families had long been problematic. Intolerance of the child by parents, inadequate parental guidance and poor family functioning were both the cause and effect of the difficult and often destructive behaviour of the children. While this pattern is typical of very disturbed children generally, some auspicious factors were found. Few children had frequently run away from home, only a handful had been rejected outright by their parents and relatives and parents were rarely described as 'over-protective'. However, the fact that the children's problems had erupted when they were relatively young raises questions about the family's ability to exert control, accept responsibility for their children's upbringing and the tendency to blame diffi-culties on external causes, such as undesirable peers and bad schools..

In summary, the family situations of the Caldecott children present a varied but generally sad picture. Although the description of individuals like Siobhan show that specific details differ from case to case and that there are many strong emotional bonds on which to build, nearly all families were characterised by a weak structure, tense relationships and stress factors. Many families like this exist across England and Wales but few have children in a place like Caldecott. It was clearly the context and combination of problems that led agencies to seek admission. It hardly needs to be said that the inability of community facilities and local schools to help the child and family had also made Caldecott a necessity.

Children's social functioning

It is often a surprise to those visiting residential child-care centres to find that the youngsters who drive staff into the ground are frequently excit-able youngsters and not the looming adolescents who, in other contexts, cause greatest concern. Any teacher knows that an unruly seven year old is quite capable of bringing everything and everyone to a halt. Caldecott children are frequently these sorts of children but their age is an asset. Staff caring for younger children tend to be more optimistic in their work than those looking after adolescents. As we shall see, Caldecott staff seek opportunities for growth and development and are less likely to use overt strategies of control and restriction. So, while all children had glaring deficiencies in their behaviour and social skills, many were also seen as likeable and able to be helped.

Nonetheless, these children still have many defects to overcome. Some of those living at Caldecott in the 1990s could not interact with others, some were uncomfortable in social situations, some were isolated, many were aggressive and a few were sexually provocative. Problems of inter-action, whether with peers or adults, and poor self-esteem had come to dominate. Complicating factors such as irritating habits, poor hygiene and hyperactivity were also frequent. Personality tests of the 60 children in our sample gave a clinical picture of immaturity, emotional disorders and lability alongside depression, poor self-image and anxiety. Thus, not only did the children come from families with a weak structure, tense relationships and multiple stress factors, but also, by the age of seven, they faced serious personal problems. In short, 'ego functioning', that mediating process central to healthy personality growth, was poor.

Naturally, family problems and poor social functioning in children are inter-related. Inconsistent parenting in a context of low warmth, high criticism and occasional abuse and neglect during infancy can lead a child to think that the world brings only badness. When this mistrust is compounded by failure and rejection, particularly at school, the likely result is poor self-esteem. These two features more than any others characterise the children arriving at Caldecott.

So much for the problems. We, like the Community staff, looked for strengths in the child's social functioning and found many. Half the children were said to be physically attractive and a quarter were described as either being clever, having good social skills or understood their situation and were able to respond to help and advice. The children were mostly amenable to treatment and were rarely victims of major illness or possible mental disorder.

In short, the problems of social functioning posed by children coming to Caldecott during the period of study were varied but not as intense as those encountered in residential institutions sheltering adolescents. Criminal convictions, attempted suicide and self-injury were rare. Conduct disorders - which have a poor prognosis and are less likely to respond to treatment - were less common than emotional disorders - which have a better outlook.

Table 4: Children's presenting behaviour on entry to the Community

	%		%
Tantrums	46	Verbal aggression	39
Destructive behaviour	44	Enuresis/encopresis	25
Disruptive behaviour	46	Delinquency	21
Physical aggression	42	Self-injury	4

We have seen that many children were referred to the Community because of their educational needs. Evidence from the previous sections may make it unnecessary to add that problems were as much to do with behaviour in school and a failure to find stability in an education context as they were to do with intellect. The following table illustrates the wide range of school difficulties which led to placement at the Community. The educational ability of residents as measured by psychometric tests was little different from that of the general population but much higher than that generally found in residential contexts for disadvantaged children. By this standard, the spread of educational performance was wide and some of the children were brighter than would have been found in Leila Rendel's day. One in six of the 60 children we considered were very able and three-quarters had an IQ score which was average or above.

Table 5: The educational problems of the children at the point of entry to the Community

	%		%
Poor behaviour in classrooms	56	Poor interaction with teachers	28
Poor interaction with pupils	47	Bullies	26
Low attainment	47	Low ability	25
Short attention span	42	Poor communication skills	16

Special difficulties of hearing and speech or of epilepsy complicated the picture for some children. A third had already been in other special educational provision and a third had been expelled from school at some point. Yet many children had aptitudes for art, reading and drama and wished to exploit these strengths. Many more children had interesting hobbies or were good with animals.

In summary this evidence again acts to remind us of the considerable disadvantages children bring with them to Caldecott. Mainstream schools had struggled to contribute to their well being. By adopting a complementary approach, the Community seeks to integrate education into work in other areas of children's lives, so producing a mutually beneficial relationship between growth and achievement. In the coming pages, we will see whether such an approach can be put into practice.

Previous involvement with statutory agencies

If Caldecott was receiving children with these deficits straight from home, its task would be difficult enough. But most had already failed in some previous intervention, many in other residential and foster care settings. Even by the age of ten, child guidance or the schools' psychological services had been involved in over four-fifths of cases and two-fifths of the children had been seen by a psychiatrist. One in six had received some psychotherapy. Application papers were littered with the assessments of professionals. Children's disadvantage was evident from the finding that two-thirds of the children had been looked after by a local authority, a third of them on more than one occasion. Of those looked after on admission to Caldecott, just over half were on care orders. Parents' unwillingness or inability to care for their offspring, neglect and abuse were the most frequent reasons for children being looked after.

This evidence shows that many Caldecott entrants are no strangers to separation. A third had been previously fostered and nearly a half had lived in community homes. These figures are surprisingly high given the young ages of the children. Generally, separations had been relatively short, less than one year on average, but four children had already lived away from home for at least five years before coming to Caldecott. No less than 30% of entrants had already spent more than a quarter of their lives living away from home.

Realistic expectations for children's futures

By the time children enter Caldecott, they have long been displaying behaviour problems. This does not always indicate long care careers. Neither does it mean that they have very severe or grave problems. The majority of the children we surveyed were diagnosed as having an emotional disorder which should improve with age and respond to treatment, albeit over a lengthy period. There are also some children with conduct disorders some of whom are highly likely to display problems of aggression and delinquency. For them, it will be harder to find a way forward. A few displayed exceptional features. For example, in one family there had been a triple infanticide and another had parents who were addicted to heroin.

The complexity of children's difficulties made expectations for the future vague. Certainly, social workers and education experts expected the children to stay long, with three-quarters having a place guaranteed for two years at the point of entry. It was hoped that the Community would focus on the child's individual needs and, in half of the 60 cases, that the family would be closely involved in this process. Within this general aim, however, there were seldom specific goals. Naturally the child's social functioning and education were mentioned, as was a desire for stability to compensate for a turbulent history, but placement at the Community was seldom linked to associated expectations for the child after Caldecott or during adulthood.

Indeed, professionals outside of the Community pre-occupied with the next difficult case frequently seemed uninterested in the child's long-term life chances. Only half thought that the child would return home but in only four cases was the social worker certain that the child could not be reunited with relatives. Most (44%) simply did not know where the child would go. From a research perspective, outcomes for troubled children are fairly predictable and it is our hope that we can use such information to better target Caldecott's scarce resources. For example, there are some children currently placed at the community who cannot benefit and there could be better matching of intervention and need for others.

Many of the features of children's lives described in this chapter are linked. So, behaviour problems at home frequently correspond with behaviour problems at school. By looking carefully at children's overlapping needs and by charting how these have changed over time, we concluded that there are four groups of children coming to Caldecott, each with its own background, treatment requirements and likely outcomes. Because of the longitudinal nature of the data collected, we can explore the interaction between the presenting problems and interventions offered, thus charting a child's life 'career', a concept which we have used successfully in several other Dartington research studies.

The first group are very young *children from fragmented families*. Such children have suffered prolonged emotional maltreatment and have endured difficult family circumstances, including several moves between relatives. Their situation has been little improved by prolonged support from social and psychological services. Many of these children will have suffered emotional abuse and frequently neglect or physical maltreatment. Sexual abuse is not, however, an issue for this group. It is to be expected that children will maintain family links in the long-term and that some will return to their relatives. As we shall explain later, if children from fragmented families benefit from stability in living and school situations, the prognosis should be good. Just over a third (35%) of the 60 children were on this career route, one of whom was Tony Bozzi described in the previous section.

The second group comprises *victims of chronic sexual abuse*. Such children will frequently have been long known to support agencies and, while they may be very bright, their schooling is likely to have been disrupted.

Apart from the abuse, their families may be functioning relatively well and if the perpetrator(s) is removed or receives treatment, the chance of a successful reunion should be high. The prognosis for such children depends much on Caldecott's ability to diagnose and respond sympathetically to the abuse and to build self-esteem, not least through attention to the child's education. Of the 60 children studied, 15% could be said to be victims of chronic sexual abuse as can Siobhan Kelly.

The third career route consists of *children with behavioural difficulties* whose problems have become manifest in an educational context. These cases share a history of educational under-achievement, disruption and exclusion from primary and special school settings. They are difficult and, if they do not already display a conduct disorder, it will be there in embryo. Mostly boys, these children have experienced a highly disrupted school life but, although they will have been separated from home, they are unlikely to have experienced multiple movements and placement breakdowns. The prognosis for these children again depends on their finding stability and on the Community's ability to engage with the family - where most will eventually reside. Of the 60 children we scrutinised, 33% were to be found on this career route, including Kevin Clarke in Woodside.

Finally, there are children whose homes are chaotic, inadequate and neglectful. The family situation is so poor that the children are already *long-term protection cases* and have experienced disruption away from home as well as within it. These children will not settle down easily and will have experienced several care placements by the time they arrive at Caldecott. Families are actively criminal and domestic violence, hostility to social services and even drug abuse also feature. It is vital that Caldecott hangs on to them, because if they leave the Community under a cloud in adolescence, their long-term prognosis will be bleak indeed. Talking to the family, getting them to understand how they contributed to the child's difficulties and giving the child a secure base to explore his or her own predicament may well hold the key to future progress. Thankfully, only 16% of the 60 children were on this career pathway. Keith Taylor, mentioned in the previous section, is a good example of children in this group.

Conclusion

We have seen how Caldecott has adapted to the needs of children in the 1980s and 1990s. It is providing a service for a small group of younger children who have educational as well as care needs. Such children need intensive and individual care; it is likely that they will respond well to a therapeutic context with a strong educational programme. It is a tribute to the Community's achievement that, while residential care and specialised psychological services for such children have declined, Caldecott continues as a successful regional resource.

We have noted that the children studied had a variety of family, social and educational problems. They brought to Caldecott considerable baggage from home and other substitute care settings. Expectations for their future were few; Caldecott was often something of a stop-gap, a place to calm the child down, to give all the chance to think and reflect. We suggest that expectations could be much more than this. Forecasting human behaviour is fraught with difficulty but to place children in a residential school without intended plans is a recipe for 'drift'. Four career routes have been identified which give some indication of the child's future life chances and the most likely strategies for improving them. Later we will add detail to this picture by proposing the most effective treatment programme to meet their needs.

We can test these ideas by following up the children after leaving Caldecott. For now, let us end this section on a note of cautious optimism. While children on any of these career routes are hardly likely to become model citizens in our post-welfare world, with the right help they should be able to find some stability, insight into their predicament, educational achievement and a modicum of happiness. If these are the standards, Caldecott should be able to help all of the children we have been discussing.

Part Four
Life in Caldecott

"

The disclosure

Early in the study we learnt that Siobhan had been sexually abused, however it was some time before she fully disclosed this to people at Caldecott. The research has shown that disclosure is a process not an event, often lasting many months and, in this instance, many years. In this section, we describe this process through excerpts from Siobhan's diary. There are no lurid details of the abuse; these are incidental to Siobhan's recovery. What we have are a few snatches of life in one part of the Community and one child's attempt to effectively use its resources.

We have selected about five per cent of the first half of Siobhan's diaries – we will use a similar proportion of material from the second half later in this study. The selection is not random. We have chosen those days which best capture Siobhan's life in Woodside, including its ups and downs. Indeed, one of the principal findings to emerge from this evidence is how development in a therapeutic context is a series of ever increasing highs interspersed with hopefully decreasing lows. There seems no place for uninterrupted improvement in a creative child-care context.

The reader will be struck – as were we – by a number of general points from Siobhan's writings. The first is the effects the struggle to disclose has upon other parts of her life. Her day-to-day mood, her ability to participate and function within the classroom, her health and relationships with home are all affected by her feelings about the abuse. It seems hardly worth saying that there is a reason for children's misbehaviour or depression but, in the hubbub of daily life of a residential institution we can sometimes forget their underlying needs. The extracts from Siobhan's diary capture these difficulties very well and provide strong evidence of the sensitivity of Caldecott staff.

Conversely, life within the Community has a considerable effect upon Siobhan's ability to disclose her abuse and come to terms with associated difficulties. The arrival and departure of members of staff is shown to have a marked effect upon the mood of the 'group' and Siobhan's inner feelings. The behaviour of the other children also plays its part. In the coming pages we get a rare glimpse of one child coming to terms with her problems. But there are other children in Woodside going through exactly the same process; Billy, Brian, Tina, Tony, Keith, Kevin, Mandy and Hayley – all struggling like Siobhan.

Life outside the Community also has its influence. The diary excerpts leave little doubt about the enduring influence of the family upon children's lives. Siobhan has been abused by several relatives and contact with her father and older brothers has been severed. Yet she desperately wants to stay in touch with brother Nigel who left home at the same time and at one point mourns her grandfather who died several years ago. Clearly contact, or its absence, has its influence upon Siobhan's well-being and the disclosure has its effects upon Siobhan's relationship with Nigel.

Other issues emerge from the following excerpts. The task of keeping children occupied, of making sure they have something to do on a rainy day and go to school when they do not want to get out of bed, is terribly important. Siobhan also reminds us of the difficulties of control. At different points she swallows glass, hovers on the edge of her second floor bedroom balcony and, most dangerous of all, hangs by her hands from a motorway bridge. She runs away, stays out all night and is frequently restrained to prevent both damage to herself and the Woodside fabric.

Each of these events can be explained by the context in which they occur. Only by providing a continuous, warm, supportive environment can the Community cope with the problems of control that Siobhan poses. Some aspects of best practice in these fraught situations can be written down in guidance and procedures but others can only be addressed by attention to the ethos and beliefs of the institution. Much will also depend upon the support given to staff. Siobhan is a lovely girl but, as she struggles to come to terms with her past, even she has the ability to exhaust the patience of the most committed carers.

These are just some of the issues to emerge from Siobhan's diary. No doubt the reader will see much more. We begin on the 8th of July, a few weeks prior to Siobhan's first anniversary at Caldecott.

8th of July

Today was a big day. I went to see my brother and all went well. We were both very pleased to see each other and were looking forward to future visits. I hope they will be more regular. Went to the sports hall when I came back. Went to bed, I've got a sore throat, probably have a cold tomorrow.

10th of July

Today was OK. I managed school in the morning, but I was a bit grumpy in the afternoon and also at lunchtime. After school we had a group meeting. The children and adults had a go at Billy and Brian Adams for their behaviour. I was tempted to muck around in the evening but I didn't. I went out on Tina's bike for a little while. I read a story to Tony. Settled well.

16th of July

Didn't manage very well today. I was stroppy and angry all day. In the evening the whole group went to do sport at Ashford grounds. I didn't want to go but I had no choice. I waited in the van with Jenny and was very upset and low. When we got back everyone watched *Ghost* but I didn't want to so I stayed in my room having a sulk. Jenny came up to see me and I came very close to speaking to her about my problem, but I didn't quite manage it. Not a very good day, although I saw Kate's flat today at lunchtime for the first time.

19th of July

Today was quite bad. I managed school although I have been stroppy all day. After school Tina and I ran off together around the grounds, even though the adults caught us almost straight away. When we got back to the group I had to sit at the homework table for about an hour and mucked around. Kate took me into the playroom and talked to me. She then left me on my own to think. I didn't want to be in there. When it was time to get changed I went upstairs and went straight to bed. I feel as though the adults are just ignoring me at the moment. Quite a bad day. PS here is poem I wrote today

Misery!
Boredom!
The rain patting the windows
The clock ticking and ticking

Thumbs twiddling
Feet tapping
Inside I am screaming
No more of this
No more of this
Computer lines
TV soaps
Breakfast, dinner and tea
School group
Group school
School group
Ghoul soup
Another spoonful
Take the medicine
Feeling better?
Just miserable!

Written by Siobhan Kelly, aged 13.

20th of July

Today wasn't that good either. I was OK for most of the day except for the evening. In the afternoon I went into town with the group. I bought Katrina's leaving presents, as she is leaving on Wednesday. I was OK when we arrived back it was just that I started mucking around towards bedtime. The adults are expecting me to do some talking but I don't think I will be able to but will probably have to sort out this problem by myself. We have got a charter meeting tomorrow. We have one four times a year. They are quite boring.

24th of July

Today was a sad day for me. Katrina left. And it is quiet without her but it was pretty upsetting to see her going. I managed the day well considering we didn't do nothing all day because of the weather. In the evening we watched a video it was quite good but I have seen it before. Managed well at bedtime. Tried to phone my brother Nigel today but he wasn't in. I'm inviting him next Monday to Hayley's 18th birthday. Everyone was allowed to invite one person and I chose Nigel. It will be three weeks on Monday since I've seen him. It seems longer than that. I'm only supposed to see him once a month so the adults have to check with Sheila my social worker. A good day I suppose.

26th of July

Today was an excellent day. We went to Folkestone and went around the shops and then we went to the Rotunda, we had a brilliant day. We got back and just hung around the front having play fights with Tony with Tristan Potter. I then phoned my brother and he was actually in (hooray). He is coming on Monday at 3pm and leaving at 9pm. I'm looking forward to it. Six hours is the longest visit I've had with Nigel since I've been here.

It's one year since I've been here, tomorrow. Yippee!

27th of July (Anniversary)

Today was another excellent day. Tina, Mandy and I went to Kate's flat and I had my hair permed, which I've been waiting for since I came here. People say it looks nice. After that we went into town, bought Hayley's present, came back and Kate let us stay up until 12.10am. We watched videos. It was a good day. It feels weird that I've actually been here for a whole year. When I first came I thought I would have left within a couple of months. I think I've improved over the last year and I'm now a much happier and politer girl. I've asked children what they thought of me when I first came here, and what they think of me now. Most of them said they prefer me now, but I was OK when I first came. A good anniversary.

6th of August

This morning didn't get off to a very good start. I ran off and headed for the shops but on the way I bumped into Zoe and I gave her a hard time. After a long while I got brought back to the group. I had to go upstairs with Mandy and I was okish. My social worker came with my new social worker. Had a good afternoon. Did some drawing and that's all. I managed the rest of the evening well. Settled to bed well by about 11.30. Quite a good day apart from the morning.

13th of September

Well today was Friday the 13th and was a very sad day for me and everyone in the group. Had a good day in school. My ankle is still hurting so I was limping all day. After school, we had a group meeting. Kate announced that Derek, Steve and Vick were all leaving. Steve on 25th of September. Vick on the 9th of October and Derek on the 1st of November. There was a very sad atmosphere in the group all evening. I went shopping with Jenny. Settled to bed well. A sad day. I feel sorry for Billy Adams.

21st of September

Mucked around all day. Went to Canterbury. Mucked around until 1.30am. Kate had to sleep in with Zoe. Adam came for a visit. I hate him but I think he's going to work here.

8th of October

This morning the adults didn't get me up. When I finally awoke I was told I couldn't go on the *Horse of the Year Show* (a school trip) because of my behaviour. I was a bit annoyed about this. Mucked around all morning but managed the afternoon and evening quite well. Did my room. Tony had his birthday party he seemed to enjoy it. I settled to bed well.

19th of October

Well today started off good but ended bad. I went to the girls' football day. When I got back Kirstie said that I was silly on the way back in the van and I didn't think I was so I wasn't allowed out. I went out anyway and stayed out all night. I feel pretty bad.

31st of October

This morning a police lady came to see me about the incident on the 19th of October when I stayed out all night with Kevin and Mark. She kept on asking me silly questions and I got a bit angry. The adults reckon I haven't taken any responsibility for it, when the day after I felt really bad. And they know that. Anyway, because of my attitude she may be coming again. We watched a video. In the evening we went to a so called Halloween party at Kitty's* house. The word 'Halloween' wasn't even mentioned. We weren't even allowed to dress up or wear masks or any-thing in case the little ones got scared. I thought this was a load of crap because the youngest child in the group is Anthony who is ten years old and I don't think he would be scared. Anyhow, we played babyish party games all evening. It was dead boring.

7th of November

Today was bad. I didn't make it into school all day. I came very close to jumping off the balcony a number of times today. In the evening we

* Kitty is Woodside's 'Granny', a role explained in later sections

A Life Without Problems?

had a group meeting. This morning Tony ran off and stole Susan's bike. The adults had a go at him in the meeting. He didn't show any remorse about what he had done. In the meeting everyone discussed their sad feelings about Derek leaving. After the meeting I was in a bad state and headed for the balcony again. I was just hanging on when Kate came and grabbed me around the wrists so I couldn't slip. I eventually came down and I was really crying. Kate gave me a long cuddle and spoke to me till I had almost stopped crying. I then went upstairs and did my room. When I got into bed I was crying again. Kate came upstairs and cuddled me for another long while and then talked to me. She said that we will have to continue our conversation from Monday, tomorrow after breakfast but before school. I was supposed to be going to the dentist tomorrow first thing but it clashes with my riding lesson, so I don't think I will be going. Couldn't get to sleep until very late again.

10th of November

Today was bad. I was pissing around all day. I scratched my arms up quite badly. We played darts and later went to the sports field and went onto the new things in the fitness centre room.

13th of November

Another bad day. Mucked around all day. Still didn't go to school. In the evening we had a group meeting and some people discussed some of their bad past experiences. I feel really pissed off and I hate this place at the moment.

17th of November

Today was quite good. I went to chapel in the morning and it was boring as usual. Managed the rest of the day OK. Played lots of darts tournaments it was good. Brett came for a visit today. He was a lanky lad and had big ears. I didn't I like him. Had my special food from Stella. Settled to bed well. Looking forward to going back to school.

21st of November

Today was bad. In the morning I went to the dentist and had a filling replaced. My mouth is now hurting. I had two injections. I managed school in the morning. In the afternoon there was no school for the seniors because the teachers were having a meeting about exams. I managed the afternoon. In the evening I was messing around. I was climbing out of windows, hanging off ledges and scratching my arm. I cried a lot in my room. Didn't get to sleep but didn't keep anyone else awake for a change. I hope to go to school tomorrow if I am in a fit state. PS Darren is starting to work here on Monday. He seems quite nice.

28th of November

Yet another bad day. Had a good day at school although I pissed about in the group. Kate held me for about three hours in the evening. I cried myself to sleep again. I hate it here. It's shit. Nigel phoned. We didn't have any arguments.

29th of November

I made it into school in the morning but not in the afternoon. It was Richard Edward's birthday today (39th). Kate held me at lunchtime. I had some glass in my mouth. Shirley from Mayfield looked after me in the afternoon. We played snooker. Kirstie and Stella held me in the late afternoon. In the evening I visited the William Harvey because I swallowed some glass. I was OK though. I arrived back at about 12am. Went straight to bed.

30th of November

A bad day. Mucked around for most of the day. In the evening I swallowed some more glass. I went down to the hospital but this time I got admitted to the Children's Ward. It is possible that I may have an operation, but there is a chance it may 'come out' naturally. Kate and Peter eventually left the hospital about 12.45am.

4th of December

Quite bad. Didn't make it into school all day. An adult had to be with me all day, in case I did anything silly. In the evening we were supposed to have a group meeting but I was refusing to sit in a certain place so I had to leave the meeting. I settled to bed quite well I suppose. Kate said she's going to have to take a statement about sexual abuse soon. She tried the other night when I was at her house. I feel very bad about myself. I know the adults are really trying to help me through this, but this is the worst I've ever been. Jenny and Kate particularly are spending lots of time with me. And I should be sorting myself out with all these people around me trying to help. I will try to do my statement tomorrow. I badly need to do something to make myself feel better.

9th of December

Today was excellent, I had my review and it went well. I spent £15 on presents for people. I bought my clothes for the Christmas party which is next Monday. I got a white top with black culottes along with various other bits and pieces. It looks very smart. I met Diane today (my old foster parent). She said I had really changed. I also met Linda, Steve and Lorna, some of my mum's friends who I spent a lot of time with in my late childhood. Settled to bed well after wrapping presents. Here are the decisions made in my review; 1) I will be staying at Caldecott until 16/17 years of age. 2) Will continue to have no further access to Kirk, Dad or Noreen Innis. 3) At the moment it isn't right for me to have contact with mum, maybe in the future. 4) I will continue to see Nigel but hopefully on a regular basis. 5) I will hopefully have contact with Adrian when a few things have been sorted out between us. 6) I will hopefully have contact with Barry if he is willing. 7) I won't be going to mainstream yet but it is an aim for the near future. 8) As from now my surname is YATES, but not quite officially yet!

11th of December

Quite a good morning in school. An awful afternoon though. Managed the evening. Had a group meeting. After the meeting I phoned Nigel. We had a massive row about the disclosures I've recently been making. He's angry with me and reckoned that I ruined Christmas. I may be seeing him next Thursday, if we are speaking to each other. He's having another review tomorrow and he says he will phone me at lunchtime to let me know what happens. I've still got a sore throat. Settled to bed quite well. I cried myself to sleep. The class are going to get a lecture from Peter Daish tomorrow about our bad behaviour.

Monday 6th January

I was depressed all day. But I was worried about tomorrow. Also it is five years today since my Granddad died. I remember him very well. I use to spend a lot of time with him and I have good memories of him. In the evening I cried in my bed. Kate is not going to be here tomorrow but Jenny will be. I want to go in by myself, but the law may say that a woman has to sit in. If so, Shirley who I have a good relationship with may come down. She is an adult from Mayfield. I stayed awake all night.

Tuesday 7th January

DC Morgan came at about 10.30am. First of all he spoke to Kate (she did decide to come in!). Then he took a statement from me while Kate was in the room as well. He was quite a nice man. He asked some very difficult questions but Kate said I managed them very well although I have my doubts. He's going to come down in about two weeks time when I've done some more work with Kate. He went about 1.30pm. In the afternoon Kate took me to her house to have some breathing space. I had a good evening watching my Salt n Pepa video and going for a ride into Ashford with Jenny. It was planned that me and Nigel could go to Folkestone Rotunda at the weekend. I phoned him to tell him but he is going home at the weekend (again). I had a massive row with him. He knew about today and gave me grief about not believing me about things about my mum. I was very upset afterwards. I couldn't tell Jenny. I settled to bed quite well considering I'm so upset.

Friday 10th January

Today was alright. I had horse riding in the morning and it was OK. I managed at lunchtime. Spent my evening in the group with Jenny. Tony was being a prat. I tidied my room before bedtime. Settled well.

Monday 13th January

Today was shit. I only just made it into school today. Lunchtime I scratched my arms up badly. I continued to mess around all day. At bedtime I spoke a little a bit to Kate about my problem about my family and about Nigel not believing me. I felt better afterwards and settled down to bed quite well. I will try to have a better day tomorrow (with any luck).

Friday 17th January

Today was crap. I had a shitty day in school. In the evening I went for a walk and decided to hang off the motorway bridge. It was a stupid thing to do. After about 10 minutes a policeman came. He got over the other side where I was. I was in a really bad state and crying and shouting. I finally half came over and was half dragged over by Darren, Ben and the policeman. I was still in a bad state when I came back. I had to stay in the staff room all evening. First of all Steve had to look after me then Jenny then Kate came in the end.

Saturday 18th January

Today I ran off with Tony. We left early in the morning. We got to Charing Cross and didn't get past the barriers. We were dumped in a detention cell until Kate and Richard came to collect us; Ben held me down in the evening and I smashed the side of my head on the radiator.

Sunday 2nd February

Another day which was good. The Archbishop of Canterbury came and we had loads of photos taken. After lunch I helped Keith Taylor to tidy his room. Later in the afternoon Kate took us for a walk. First of all we went to a farm and saw loads of baby lambs. Then we went to a restaurant. It was good fun. In the evening Kate took us for a walk over to the playground. We had a good game of football. I accidentally kicked Kate in the foot. She's got a swollen leg now. Kate spent some time with me in the evening. Settled to bed well. We've got no school tomorrow (boring!).

Saturday 8th February

An excellent day. We went Maidstone. We split into groups. Anthony and I had to go with Kate. I got some new clothes and some school shoes. It was good fun. On the way back we went to Kitty's house to pick up Billy who had stayed there for the day. We stayed there for a little while and had a drink. We got back quite late. Tina had a massive paddy then Tony went out of the group. The adults had to stay back really late because they couldn't find him. I settled to bed well after watching TV till quite late. A good day.

Wednesday 12th February

Today was quite bad. I wasn't very good in school in the morning. At lunchtime I was in a right old sulk. In the afternoon I refused to do any work, so Richard Edwards phoned up Kate and she came and collected me. I stayed in my room all afternoon. In the afternoon (I mean evening) I went off to school and apologised to Richard for my behaviour. When I came back we had a group meeting. I settled to bed well. PS DC Morgan is coming on Friday 21st February: Keith Taylor's birthday and the day we break up from school.

Conclusions

The diary excerpts illustrate the underlying factors behind apparently illogical demanding behaviours. Many residential centres and foster homes will be faced with situations such as those described by Siobhan. In other respects, she is unusual and her contribution untypical. Very few in residential care share Siobhan's characteristics and only a tiny proportion experience an environment like Caldecott. (After all, how many children in care have met the Archbishop of Canterbury!). But all children in places like Caldecott or in foster homes have problems and, like Siobhan will be struggling to come to terms with them.

Siobhan has much going for her. She is attractive and clever – a pleasure to be with. Not all children looked after have these attributes; protective factors, as a clinician would refer to them. Not all children benefit from the continuous concern and insight of a few dedicated members of staff. Even within Caldecott, the quality of care offered within Woodside is exceptional. With these advantages, Siobhan has struggled to get insight into her problems. The process of disclosure has been difficult and possibly mistakes were made along the way. But 18 months after entry she has a firm base on which to build a future life. We will see how she progresses later in the study. But before then we need to consider the types of treatment available for children like Siobhan both within the Community and elsewhere.

Treating troubled children

Caldecott is a therapeutic community. For some, this description reveals all about life in the Adam house near Ashford but for others the psychological nomenclature obscures the nature of the work. Few outsiders find it easy to grasp how the theoretical principles which guide Caldecott's work are applied in practice. Indeed, as we shall see, many inside the Community are similarly unsure and nowhere is its treatment approach clearly written down. Unfortunately, in this respect, Caldecott is no different from most other residential child-care centres. In this section we seek initially to provide a description of different approaches to troubled children that is comprehensible to a lay person. We next build into this discussion some observations about Caldecott's work and suggest ways in which its intervention might influence the children's career routes described earlier. It is intended that this section will be relevant to those seeking to provide a viable regime in childrens homes and residential schools. Those wishing for a deeper analysis will want to turn to the standard texts laid out in the references.

The behaviour displayed by Siobhan during her first 18 months in Woodside may be regarded as indicating some form of psychological difficulty. We knew the origins of her unhappiness but the symptoms are of both conduct disorder (for example hanging from the motorway bridge and running away) and emotional disorder (such as the depression and mood change). We could fill this book many times over with theories for understanding and treating Siobhan's problems but we can summarise much of the evidence by focusing on two types of explanations. *Psychoanalytic* theories emphasise the importance of repressed, unconscious motives which have, if possible, to be brought to consciousness. In contrast, others working in this field stress the importance of *environmental* factors, and the way certain behaviours are learned and 'unlearned' Although Caldecott identifies more with the former, these theories are not mutually exclusive and, in our experience, a successful intervention will mix and match ideas from several sources.

Psychoanalytic explanations

Given Leila Rendel's professional associations and her continual emphasis of the child's emotional well being, it was natural that the Community should prefer a broadly psychoanalytic approach to children's problems. In this tradition, much greater salience is given to the underlying personality of the child as it develops in the first stages of life. A child's personality structure is thought to change little in its essentials from the early formative years. Stress is placed upon what Sigmund Freud termed 'intrapsychic' phenomena, those aspects of a child's early rearing which become subsumed into the unconscious but continue to influence later interaction with the family and much other behaviour. Based on an analysis of adults' memories of childhood, Freud focused upon the first six years of the child's life, defining what he called the oral, anal and genital stages of development. These theories have been subsequently developed by Anna Freud, Klein, Winnicott, Balbernie and Dockar-Drysdale, all of whom worked directly with children.

Although diverse, psychoanalytic theory always stresses the importance of past relationships upon current patterns of interaction and it is principally concerned with psychological processes in child development, such as the way we transfer emotions about one social context to other situations, a process often referred to as transference. The psychoanalytic tradition frequently uses techniques to take a child back to its infancy to uncover the roots of problems manifest in later life. This process, 'regression' as it is called, is a highly skilled task and, if poorly applied, is harmful and even abusive.

In the ideas of transference and regression, we can see the importance of inter-generational factors in psychoanalytic theory. A father's emotional abuse of his son might well reflect poor father-son relationships in previous generations. Great stress is also placed upon family relationships and, for example, sibling position. Analytic theory which attempts to explore the unconscious mechanisms that motivate behaviour has been refined by Dockar-Drysdale who identified the 'severely damaged frozen child' who had lost all capacity for emotional relationships and in the practical therapy of Balbernie who developed the concept of the 'unintegrated child', that is one who has never been able to relate the different components of personality (thus leaving the therapist with very little to work on).

Psychotherapeutic approaches

In practice, psychotherapeutic work focuses upon the 'whole child' in his or her family. The treatment seeks to understand all of the elements in the child's life and to explore the relationships between them. So, while the presenting problem of a child coming to Caldecott maybe truancy or poor interaction with peers, the treatment looks beyond these to relationships at home, in school and in the neighbourhood. The Community is also seen as a single system so that there should be consistency of approach in the living units, the school, out-reach programmes and throughout the Caldecott campus. Balbernie captured this well when he described the 'healing boundaries' which were placed around the Cotswold Community.

As we have seen, this approach to troubled children was applied in several child-care centres between the wars and again in the 1960s; indeed, some, for example Caldecott, Peper Harow and the Mulberry Bush developed international reputations for their work. While the approach of these places has never been scientifically validated, they have been pioneering, so it is sad to report that their survival is constantly under threat and that some, most notably, Peper Harow have closed.

Familiar status divisions applied in residential care are blurred within psychotherapeutic regimes. For example, members of the Community are referred to as adults and children, not as staff and residents. As we saw from Siobhan's diary, a variety of forums are established to encourage interaction and a rich environment of confrontation is fostered. Members of the Community are encouraged to interpret their own and others' behaviour. Self-monitoring extends to adults and, indeed, the residential workers often monitor the effects of individual children upon their own situation. Some staff may seek external counselling or indeed psychoanalysis in order to aid their practice. Needless to say, the intellectual, emotional and physical demands upon all those in residential centres of this kind are considerable.

The social environment at Caldecott is structured by the staff and young people are invited to join 'the group' as they feel capable. The approach is reflected in the language used; 'group-workers' attempt to provide a 'total living situation' which continuously attempts to achieve insights into the young person's life and to effect positive changes. As Siobhan's writings clearly demonstrate, progress in one area frequently heralds a crisis in another. Steady development is sometimes difficult to identify and is seldom recorded.

Caldecott functions around numerous meetings and accumulated documentary evidence on each child and 'the group'. There are weekly staff support meetings and treatment meetings between staff and residents. There are daily business meetings on each unit and 'change-over' meetings at which the progress of the group is reported. In addition, there are less frequent meetings between people in the Community and representatives from outside, for example, at six-monthly reviews. The main, some would say unfortunate, gap in this series of gatherings is any opportunity for key family members to gain insights into their own behaviour and, in turn, to comprehend their children's response. This technique, extensively employed in family therapy, is also used to some effect in other residential therapeutic settings which invite family members to stay and to participate in the child's treatment plan.

Environmental explanations

While Caldecott is primarily using psychoanalytic techniques, it is worth considering other approaches, particularly those based on environmental explanations of children's problems. Widespread experiments with animals have led psychologists to argue that human behaviour is responsive to the environment and that action can be learned and 'unlearned'. Pavlov introduced the idea of conditioning, that in certain circumstances the incidence of a particular behaviour will increase if it is followed by a reward or reinforcement and will decrease if followed by some form of punishment. Skinner developed this line of thinking with the concept of modelling. Accordingly, difficult behaviour is explained either as the failure to learn normal social skills or by the acquisition of specific deviant skills, for example, petty delinquency, often in a reinforcing cycle. Some have refined these ideas, for example, suggesting the existence of 'streetwise' skills used by some young people which are appropriate to some environments but maladaptive in others.

Simply stated, those applying this environmental model to the treatment of children seek to reinforce appropriate behaviour and to reduce inappropriate responses by withdrawing treats. In practice, such treatments tend to take three forms. Behaviour is modified by, for example, a system of punishment and rewards for specified actions. There are also social learning programmes which seek to provide children with social skills to accomplish normal behaviours and to reject opportunities to be anti-social, so breaking destructive cycles. Finally, children can be encouraged, without any direct reinforcement, to model their behaviour on the orthodox and to reap the social rewards that normally follow such actions.

Clearly, there is a lot of common-sense in this environmental model; after all, most of us adapt our own behaviour according to social rewards and punishments. The approach is wide ranging and has been applied in many contexts; indeed, success has been claimed for several groups of problem children from arsonists to bed-wetters. Positive results can be achieved rapidly. On the other hand, 'behaviourists', as they have become known, have been criticised for a failure to maintain and build upon short-term achievements and for the lack of any clear association between treatments and effects.

Social learning techniques

How are these ideas applied in practice? While a pure application of behaviourism would be anathema to Caldecott, some parts of its practice do reflect social learning techniques. In residential care, environmental explanations of children's behaviour are usually translated into social learning models. The quintessence of this model is behaviour modification, sometimes known as the 'token economy'. The basis of these schemes is that each child is held personally responsible for his or her behaviour. Increasingly demanding targets are set for each individual, and if these are reached tokens or points are gained which can be exchanged for outings, goods, sweets, shampoo or other benefits, for example, a more pleasant room.

Other methods have been incorporated into the social learning repertoire. Contracts, sometimes written out and formally signed, between staff and child have been drawn up. Programmes for developing social skills are extensively used. There are, in addition, treatment packages designed to encourage the young person to re-examine their own behaviour and to improve certain skills, for example personal hygiene and self-appearance.

Behaviour modification, like any treatment programme, can be misused and many have asked whether the use of rewards and punishments in residential settings is ethical. Critics have warned that a young person's rights should never be contingent on satisfactory behaviour. Moreover, clever children are adept at manipulating the system and 'tokens' can become part of an underground economy. Attempts at 'modelling' rest uneasily with the usual tensions about language, smoking, dress and sexual relations common in all residential settings.

On the other hand, behaviour modification encourages staff to look at the individual needs of children and to explore the intricacies of the child's pathology. The programme has been especially successful in homes specializing in work with adolescents by introducing the concept of 'reward' into settings where 'punishment' has been pervasive. It also gives a common focus for the different staff groups and stresses the importance of interaction between staff and children. Moreover, young people find it easy to understand.

Meeting the needs of Caldecott's residents

Having simply described the broad themes which underpin psychoanalytic and environmental approaches to children's problems and outlined some practical applications, it is pertinent to ask how these ideas are implemented at Caldecott.

Unfortunately, this is not an easy question to answer. The Community's approach is frequently talked about but seldom committed to paper. Distinguished thinkers are often mentioned in a reverent tone of voice, but only a small proportion of the 150 members of staff have ever read and understood the relevant texts. This is a deficiency of Caldecott's work because the dissemination of its methods would be of considerable benefit to other residential centres seeking coherence in their work.

Some of this information is conveyed in the considerable documentation that accumulates on each child but, even here, there are weaknesses. Particularly worrying can be the gap which opens between care plans for the child - a fundamental part of the residential task since the implementation of the *Children Act*, 1989 - and treatment plans fashioned at Caldecott. The reluctance to tease out specific aims and objectives for each child from the general approach to troubled youngsters at Caldecott is also of concern. We would encourage any residential centre to ask the question, 'in the context of the likely long-term outcomes for this child, what can be achieved during his or her period of residence?' The answer should be clearly documented and regularly reviewed.

Having made these criticisms of Caldecott - and by association most other therapeutic communities and residential centres - by reading childrens' files and other records, by talking to staff and children and by breathing the ether, it has been possible to identify some particular features of Caldecott's approach as it seeks to meet the general needs of children in its care. Some features apply to the work of staff and the life of the institution, others are more directly concerned with the children.

The work of staff and the life of the institution

Perhaps the first thing to be said is that Caldecott is eclectic in its approach borrowing techniques from several treatment traditions. Any residential centre requires some elements of behaviourism to make it work and children at Caldecott are certainly rewarded for good behaviour and encouraged to follow others in the Community who act as good role models. However, there is no place for tokens or scales of achievement – in a psychotherapeutic environment this would be impossible to manage – but the broad principles of the social learning approach are effectively utilised.

The Community also sets out clear expectations about staff behaviour, language and dress. The term 'projective identification' is used, which means that everything done within the Community will have some effect, either to add to or detract from children's growth and maturation. Thus, even apparently mundane aspects of the staff role, such as attention to cleanliness within the units, driving the children to different destinations and idle talk about daily life, are given greater significance than in most other residential settings.

This being so, while emphasis is placed upon the provision of a warm supportive environment, firm boundaries are placed around children's behaviour. They are, for example, expected to go to school; they wear a school uniform and when they behave badly they will be confronted by staff. Warm and supportive should not be equated with soft or easy-going. Thus, in some respects, Caldecott might be viewed as very orthodox and even authoritarian in some of its attitudes to children.

Attention is also directed to the needs of staff. In previous sections we have given vivid examples of Siobhan's panic and anxiety. For every major incident that she described, there were members of staff restraining her, tempting her back from the bedroom balcony, pulling her over on to the right side of the motorway bridge or delivering her to hospital for observation. In these circumstances, staff also panic and need considerable oversight and support.

Lastly, with regard to the work of staff and the life of the institution, there is both an integrated approach at Caldecott and some differentiation between roles. For example, the education of children is clearly part of the treatment process and the school operates so as to complement the aims and objectives of care staff. Within this continuity, staff are allocated clear tasks; to look after, to teach or to provide specialist help, for example, psychotherapy for the child.

Work with children

If staff are asked to describe the nature of the psychotherapeutic task, most will talk about the need to recreate attachments for the children and to build upon developments in this area by encouraging the explanation of painful past memories. So, once children feel secure at the Community and are clear about the limits of acceptable behaviour, they will begin to talk about previous maltreatment. This might take place in a group, in one-to-one sessions with a care worker or teacher or in consultation with one of the Community's specialists.

Children are then encouraged to identify and gain control over impulses which lead to difficult behaviour. They learn to build up defence mechanisms and to control their anxiety. In the therapeutic community this work is undertaken in group or counselling sessions but in other residential contexts the same goals are pursued by different means, for example, through a variety of social learning techniques.

Generally, Caldecott strives to be consistent in its approach to children and is aware of the mechanisms used by residents to manipulate and unsettle staff. The terms 'projection' and 'splitting' are frequently used to describe those situations which children identify and take sides with people during disputes or attempt to turn one member of staff against another. The motive for such behaviour may be unconscious to the children but the effects are real to the staff.

Meeting the individual needs of children

In seeking simple descriptions of treatment approaches, there is a danger of over simplifying the complex work being undertaken. Some have reduced the task of therapeutic communities to a single definition. Tom Main describes a psychotherapeutic environment as having a commitment to continuous

> inquiry about personal and group anxieties.... and defences, and of endeavour to create adaptive, thought-out roles, relations, structure, and culture which is geared to real tasks.... relevant to the capacities and needs of individuals.

Whether or not this definition holds for Caldecott is a matter for discussion. What we can say is that the Community should seek to measure its intervention according to the needs of each child. This should be done on a case by case basis. For ease of description, and because we believe the method can help us predict outcomes, we earlier categorised Caldecott's residents into four career routes. It will be recalled that we identified *children from fragmented families* who have suffered difficult family circumstances. There are children who have been *victims of chronic sexual abuse*, and have long been receiving help away from home. Third, we noted *children with behavioural difficulties* whose principal problems have emerged in school and *long-term protection cases* whose chaotic, neglectful parents have left them ill-equipped to cope.

What can Caldecott offer these four groups? Our observations are based on three sources of information: a close scrutiny of the situations of the 60 young people who left Caldecott between 1986 and 1990; an intensive look at 12 children entering the Community in 1990; and a long research involvement with children looked after away from home. We bring a partial perspective and some might disagree with our assessment of these children's needs. However, all would agree that some assessment of need linked to treatment intervention is required for children presenting the range and level of difficulty as those sheltered by Caldecott. The following pages seek to provide a step in that direction.

Children from fragmented families

More than most, these children need stability and security. Some would claim that those on this career route could benefit as much from placement with a family, especially one close to home. It is certainly true that these children need role models and experiences of non-abusing adults and peers. But Caldecott has an edge on this alternative by the provision of education which can add to the child's sense of stability and also raise his or her self-esteem. For this to work, however, the Community must also give the family some insight into how their social and psychological situation has contributed to the child's maltreatment. The child's absence from home will have come as a welcome period of respite for parents and it will take considerable effort to maintain links with home and relatives.

Victims of chronic sexual abuse

To an extent, we have seen how the Community approaches children on this career route. The first task with Siobhan was to give a sense that she was safe; as we shall see, this is a constant battle when children have been severely abused. The process of disclosure can, therefore, take some time and, when it occurs, continuing work sometimes focusing on further disclosures will be required. All of this must continue against the

---

backdrop of several, sometimes competing, emotions on the part of the child, particularly frustration, anger, confusion, ambivalence and distress. Siobhan's acting out can be explained but the staff still have to deal with it in a way that leaves her safe and feeling secure.

The work with the abuse must not detract from family work. Siobhan has several non-abusing relatives with whom she will want to stay in touch, not least her brother Nigel with whom she was separated from home. There will also be a need to deal with the guilt and remorse of family members (whether or not they have contributed to the maltreatment). Education to raise self-esteem and as an avenue towards normal relationships with peers and adults is also likely to pay dividends with children on this career route.

Children with behavioural difficulties

By virtue of their reasons for entering Caldecott, the primary focus of the treatment will be on the child's education. They need individual attention and encouragement to achieve in a supportive non-rejecting environment. This will mean that any disruption in the classroom can be contained, probably requiring a flexible curriculum and a stimulating school environment. A modicum of behaviour modification by way of rewards for good behaviour will certainly help in this context. Once again, we would also stress the importance of contact with family members, especially as these children are the most likely to return to live with relatives on leaving the Community.

Long-term protection cases

For these children, family work which involves the family has to be a priority. In addition, some social skills training and life enriching experiences which compensate for some of the separation that the child has previously suffered will be welcome. Love that does not displace or disenchant family members seems to be the best strategy for children on this career route. As we shall see, Caldecott is not always wholly successful in this respect.

Conclusions

It is impossible in a few pages adequately to describe the complexities of a therapeutic treatment programme. Nonetheless, we hope we have provided, in lay persons' language, a flavour of Caldecott's approach and some of the other influences upon regimes in residential communities. We have also tried to show how any treatment programme must be focused. We could not take this analysis down to the level of each individual child – something the Community must do if it is to be effective – but we have looked at different strategies for the four career routes described earlier in the study.

It is at this point that we begin to see the career routes as more than a device to describe the different experiences and needs of children at Caldecott. We would hypothesise that, given certain conditions, outcomes for children can be expected to be moderately good. Where the treatment programme focuses on the particular needs of children as we describe above; where the treatment approach encourages the child to understand the way in which the family contributed to his or her difficulty and involves the family in that process; and where goals set for the child's stay at Caldecott are followed through, we believe that outcomes – in all areas of the child's life –will be optimal.

In the coming pages we can begin to test this hypothesis by seeing what happens to the 60 children who left the Community between 1986 and 1990. A more rigorous guide will be the progress of children in the intensive study who came to Caldecott in 1990. For them we have better information on their experiences within the Community and their progress thereafter. In seeing whether our ideas hold up, we should also discover why and when Caldecott's approach fails children. We are helped in this task by a closer scrutiny of life within the eight living units that make up the Community, of which Woodside is typical.

Woodside

How are the treatment regimes just described made available for troubled children in Woodside, the unit in which Siobhan lives? Woodside has strategies to tackle the individual needs of children but for all residents it describes its aims as:

> providing the child with a safe and supportive environment that will facilitate the process of disclosure and the promotion of the child's education. Increasingly, family work is also being given the priority it deserves.

These objectives are not unlike those proposed in the previous section for children who have been victims of sexual abuse. But, will they survive in the daily whirl of life in a residential centre and will they have any effect? In this section we assess the strengths and weaknesses of the Unit in realising its objectives. We then assess the standards of care offered to the children by applying a model used in other Dartington research into residential centres around the country.

Providing a safe and secure environment

Providing children at Woodside with a stable environment is achieved in three ways: the cohesive nature of its staff group, the control exercised over the children's physical environment and behaviour, and the time and attention dedicated to residents' individual needs. In combination, these three aspects of Woodside's work should be sufficient to meet its primary objective.

Staff cohesion

The staff, known as 'adults', are mostly young and single with little, if any, previous experience of residential work. Their training is intended to teach a set of ideals, philosophy, methods and language. The hope is that a common experience will emerge, providing a united approach and a shared belief in the work. For the children this should mean that, regardless of who is on shift, the care is consistent.

Staff are quickly immersed in Caldecott. As the following sections demonstrate, shifts are very long - from seven in the morning until 10.30 at night. A normal working day involves participation in the Woodside routine from the time the children get up in the morning until way past their bed time at night. As one adult said; 'You live here and go home for a break.' Many also live in close proximity to the Community. Such intense involvement in their place of work requires a great deal of commitment to and belief in Caldecott's approach

Not suprisingly, many younger members of staff become exhausted and leave the work. Most strong units within Caldecott compensate by having one or two people who can endure the pressures and stay long. The Woodside team manager Kate Edwards has been part of the Community since 1980. She does not manage from a distance; with no separate office she is clearly part of the shift system. As Siobhan's diary has shown, Kate has a lot of involvement with the children and, like the other adults, is a key worker to two or three residents. She is also accessible to staff for supervision and support, both formal and informal. Kate Edwards and her assistant team manager, Stella, have been working together for seven years. They know each other's ways of working and provide continuity for adults and children alike – essential for the sense of safety, security and stability that prevails in Woodside.

Control

The adults control the children's physical space. A clear structure is set for the child's day, determining every part of life; times for waking, eating, education, leisure activities, washing and sleeping are all monitored. Children are not allowed upstairs on their own and at night they are obliged to inform the adult sleeping-in if they are going to the toilet. The physical boundaries are clear and set. Within them adults and children alike know what is expected; specific activities from chores in the kitchen to individual sessions in the play room all have their place and time.

It is not only the children's time and physical environment that the adults control. Their behaviour is also closely monitored, giving the impression that every look given, word said and movement made is under scrutiny. Adults consistently and openly challenge the children to stop behaving like 'pseudo-adults' or 'football louts'. Regardless of the setting, on route to the classroom or over a card-game in the lounge, the immediacy of these challenges is surprising. 'Time out' to discuss 'offending behaviour' is part and parcel of this package.

Woodside's Granny, called Kitty, untrained and in her eighties, might be expected to provide a softer, less confrontational adult figure. This is not the case. Because age brings respect, Kitty can be immediate and direct in her interactions. For example, she is quick to censure the children for not giving up their seat if a visitor walks into the room. Being one generation, if not two or three, apart from the others in Woodside neither dilutes the message nor changes the approach.

Woodside's boundaries, then, both control the physical environment and determine levels of acceptable behaviour. Within these limits the adults have high expectations of the children. Standards of hygiene and tidiness, for example, are high. As the cleaner commented, these children are much tidier and more disciplined than her own! It is against this backdrop that the intensive 'therapeutic' work takes place.

Attention to individual needs

A key goal of the Woodside treatment plan is to facilitate the disclosure of each child's maltreatment. A glance at Siobhan's diary reveals the lengthy and extremely painful nature of this process. Hence it is essential that every child within the group feels adequately supported. Important are the keyworkers, special adults from the group allocated to each child. These keyworkers take considerable responsibility, from the daily accompaniment of their child at the breakfast table to the more intensive individual work.

Keyworkers are responsible for their key child's weekly playroom sessions. These provide a forum for one-to-one interactions. In a similar vein, the child is given individual time in the evening. The keyworker will go to the child's room at bedtime and the child will have some 'special food'. This might be a bag of crisps, a cup of soup, sweets, or a bottle of milk but is always something chosen specially by the child. 'Special food' time helps in building a trusting and supportive relationship. Close adult/child relationships are encouraged as an important part of the treatment process.

We will see later that, at times, children feel estranged from the group. On these occasions, children are taken into a quiet setting for short periods. A child behaving in a manner unacceptable to the adults is said to be 'out of communication' and, in extreme circumstances, will be kept back from school and from many leisure activities. While the other children are away, quiet periods are devoted to school work or the arts and crafts. The hope is that, by providing a calm and attentive environment, any extreme behaviour will be pacified.

Consequences of the secure environment

A casual visit to any of the units at Caldecott will frequently be misleading. The impression given is of little order but it is actually a very controlling environment. Violent incidents, though they do occur, are rare. Our experience in other residential homes tells us that the adults at Caldecott are unusual in the amount of time they spend playing and interacting with the children. Unlike staff in other homes they spend relatively little time during the day shut away over paper work in the office.

Yet there are also negative consequences of this nurturing, highly protective world. Children can become isolated from the local community and their home environment, raising doubts as to their viability on leaving. Also, the adult protectors in Woodside are mainly young, single and have little experience of ordinary children. It is not unusual for the children to be challenged for behaviour that would be acceptable in other environments, for example being noisy at birthday parties and wanting to be the centre of attention, both of which could be viewed as 'normal' in children. It is not always easy for a young staff team to remember that 'damaged' children need not be treated as 'different'.

Family work

If education takes a high priority at Caldecott, then by comparison family work is relatively low on the list of concerns. We have seen that families play only a peripheral role in the treatment plan. One of the effects of creating a place of safety with clear boundaries to protect and contain the child can be to exclude the outside world. Regardless of their backgrounds, children's birth families naturally remain important to them. They take great care and pride in compiling life story books and family photograph compilations. They are encouraged by the adults in this documentation of their 'roots', so why is it that families remain so marginal?

The adults will explain that the distances involved in working with families stand in the way of contact. The telephone can be used, and the children can receive calls but these are monitored and are restricted to convenient times. On one girl's birthday, a call came through from her brother and sister in South America, several time zones away, yet they were told to telephone back later at a better time for the unit. There is a feeling that the child has become a member of the Caldecott family, which is placed before the family of birth. Whilst it is not voiced, there is an underlying sense that parents must be blamed for the child's problems. It is not surprising that the adults, having developed strong bonds with the children in their care, feel protective.

Education

Located a few yards from the mansion house, Caldecott's own school is in converted stables and coach houses around a series of courtyards. The poor educational performance of looked after children has been the source of considerable concern over recent years, yet Caldecott manages this part of its caring task well. What features of the education work contribute to this success? Firstly, and most simply, children are expected to go to school, either within the Community or to mainstream establishments outside. Every unit is responsible for ensuring that children are tidily dressed in school colours and every morning several crocodile lines emerge from the main door of the mansion house and amble across the front lawns to their appropriate destinations.

Secondly, within the Community's own school, classrooms are differentiated according to their task, as well as the child's age and educational ability. For example, there are 'nurture' classes which help prepare pupils for ordinary school life and some otherwise orthodox classes have 'nurture corners' which give the less secure children some respite from the normal routine. In addition to the teachers, most of whom have long experience with special needs children, there are support assistants who offer general help and keep the class going if the teacher gets caught up with a recalcitrant child. In very difficult situations, care staff will also be called into the classroom to help calm a pupil and occasionally children will be taken back to their living unit until they have quietened down.

The attention to the emotional support of the children does not, however, mean that educational needs are neglected. The Caldecott school operates the National Curriculum and the standard range of subjects is available. Expectations for pupils are high and aim towards standard assessments and public examinations. Homework is set and time is allocated within the living units for its completion. Lessons are not seen as a privilege they are viewed as a right and as integral to children's long term development.

Since many of the children arrive at Caldecott with a history of educational problems, changing their negative attitude towards school is fundamental to the teachers' work. Children are therefore kept back from school on arrival at Caldecott and work in structured sessions with a keyworker takes place in the living unit. It may be some weeks before a child is considered able to cope in a classroom setting. The incentives for children to get to school are manifest. Educational problems, school exclusion and truancy are common among children in residential care whereas at Caldecott going to school is accorded high status.

For all children, contact between the adults who look after them and the school they go to is important. At Caldecott, adults from each unit escort their children to and from school morning and evening, as well as collecting them for a meal in the main building at lunch time. Four times daily, therefore, adults and teachers meet and share information on each child's behaviour and achievements. If a child is not coping well in school during the morning, something can be done at lunch. But it is not only the negative aspects of work and behaviour that will be passed on; approval for good school work is also given generously by adults and children alike.

The ultimate aim of the Caldecott school is to provide education that will enable each child to fulfil his or her full potential. For some this will mean a move into mainstream education, a policy encouraged by school inspectors in the late 1980s, and, for a handful, transfer to day special schools for children with learning difficulties. There are several ordinary schools in the Ashford area each with different strengths. The transfer can lead to worries and problems, one of which is the antagonism shown towards the 'leaver' by the other children at Caldecott. Children's conflicting emotions – sadness at the loss of a school friend; pleasure for the friend who has made such progress; jealousy perhaps as well as fear – can seriously threaten the success of the move.

Finally, in addition to formal educational needs, Caldecott puts great emphasis on a child's wider cultural and other social needs. All children receive lessons in riding, stable management and the care and feeding of ponies. Cookery, art and pottery are also available at the school. Trips to museums, art galleries, plays and films are frequent. Once again, it is the attention to detail that attracts attention.

Assessing the effectiveness of Woodside

We have described the way in which Woodside implements treatment plans and how Caldecott provides education for troubled children. We have hinted at strengths and weaknesses in this approach but some reading this report will be left asking whether Caldecott's strategy is any more effective than that of other residential settings. At Dartington, we have studied nearly 200 residential centres over three decades, an experience which has given some insight into the conditions that make for good residential care. Successive studies have improved our understanding in this area and in *Residential Care for Children: A Review of the Research* we stated that effective residential care has the following features:

- Children feel enriched by the residential experience and perceive some caring role.
- Children see themselves as acquiring clear instrumental skills during their stay.
- The residential establishment pursues a set of goals which are matched to the primary rather than the secondary needs of children; for example, the needs which necessitated absence from home rather than those, such as control, brought about by living in residential care. These are reiterated in a wide variety of ways and permeate the whole control process.
- Effective organisations demonstrate some consensus amongst staff, children and parents about what these goals should be and how they should be achieved. To maintain this consensus, leadership is clear and consistent. Staff are reminded of the strengths of residential care as well as warned against its weaknesses.
- The establishment makes efforts to fragment the informal world of the children by a variety of structural features. This is achieved by creating small group situations, by giving older children responsibility or by encouraging close staff/child relationships.

Do these conditions apply in Woodside and other parts of the Caldecott Community? Siobhan's diary suggests that children are enriched by their stay. She tells us of the warmth and concern shown by the adults towards all the children who feel 'cared for'. Each child has at least two people to turn to for help, two people who can swap roles between confrontation and comfort.

It also provides instrumental skills. Gaining an education is an obvious area, but the children in Woodside are also encouraged to improve their social and communication skills. The children are constantly encouraged to express their thoughts and opinions. They are corrected when they behave unacceptably and are rewarded when they show good manners.

Are the goals of Woodside matched to the primary needs of the children? This is Caldecott's strongest dimension. While there are strategies to cope with the secondary needs of children living in a residential centre, not least those of control, there are in place a range of specific tools aimed at helping children come to terms with their maltreatment or other disadvantage. The consistent and united adult approach, and the use of various therapeutic tools such as 'special food' and being 'out of communication', the emphasis on education; with the exception of close attention to the child's home circumstances, everything in Woodside and in other parts of the Community is aimed at the primary need of the child

If Caldecott is strong when measured against the first three criteria in the model, holes in the Woodside blanket of care begin to show when we consider the consensus of aims and methods between adults children and family. It is certainly true that the children and adults, and, to an extent, the field social worker, know and agree upon why the child is in Woodside. The admission process is lengthy, well documented and involves visits by the child to meet the adults and children. The child's understanding of and agreement to the placement is considered most important by the adults.

The Community has adopted an approach to its residents which might be described as an open residential adoption. It admits children and, if they respond to the treatment intervention, like Trevor described in the opening sections of this book, it will provide support well into adulthood. However, just as those who study adoption have questioned the need for permanent family placements to be exclusive and to exclude outsiders, so it might be opportune for Caldecott to consider its relationship with the world beyond its walls. Communication with other organisations struggling with many of the same problems may well be rewarding.

Adults in Woodside are always aware of children's potential to undermine the carefully organised therapeutic process and have, therefore, developed elaborate strategies to fragment the informal world of children. In contrast to other children's homes, keeping control of the child group does not command undue time and concern. We have seen that the children are carefully supervised throughout all their waking hours, a tight rein justified by the children's potential for self-harm or abuse.

Management of the children's informal world is a sensitive process, as we can illustrate with evidence from one of the weekly children's meeting. These meetings are for the children, although adults also attend. Towards the end of her stay, Siobhan was joined in Woodside by Hayley who was initially highly disruptive. In their meeting, the children challenged Hayley about her behaviour. The group demands prevailed and

Hayley's pattern of misbehaviour ended. This one incident shows not only the power of a cohesive child culture to influence each other but also the subtlety of management of a difficult pattern of child behaviour by the adults.

Using this model, we can see the strength of Woodside and the areas of possible improvement. Other residential centres can gauge their contribution against these criteria. Each study of residential care has led us to adapt this model. Our experience at Caldecott is no exception. At the Community, we have been struck by the value of a shared belief in residential care. Beleaguered, in the current child-care environment, most residential homes seldom have such conviction. The few that have cohesive staff groups, an understanding of aims and methods and information about outcomes for children tend to be those that prosper. Belief, therefore, may be an additional factor to look for when assessing residential care and predicting outcomes. The presence of a consistent, respected leadership throughout a residential centre is a necessary condition for the transmission of such a belief system.

Table 6: Conditions for good residential care: their presence in Woodside

Conditions	Woodside's response	Conditions present
Enrichment	Children consider they are cared for and cared about by adults.	✓
Acquire skills	Children improve social skills and education.	✓
Goals match primary needs.	General aim to help children cope with abuse.	✓
Consensus of views with children. staff social worker and family.	Adults, children and social worker agree upon aims and methods.	✓
	Family peripheral, though some efforts are made.	✗
Staff aware of and seek to control informal child world.	Children closely supervised so staff aware of informal worlds. Groups managed by staff. Child world used to control behaviour.	✓

Working at Caldecott

The preceding pages should begin to indicate the types of children living at Caldecott and the way in which the Community responds to their deficits. We have talked abstractly about Caldecott's work, almost as if children's problems were a puzzle waiting to be solved. As Siobhan's diary entries testify, the reality is more complex and much depends upon the commitment and understanding of the people who work there. We next consider their circumstances, aspirations and frustrations.

Staffing at children's homes has been a topical issue over the last five years. The reports of Utting, Warner, Howe, Levy and Kahan have all focused on the problems of recruitment, retention and supervision of trained residential social workers and their poor conditions of service. Two of the reports emerged as a result of maltreatment of children by staff and findings have noted the importance of creating the necessary conditions for high quality care. Much has been written about the lack of recognition given to those who work in residential contexts and the dwindling support for their task from the public, allied professions and managers.

We need not rehearse these arguments for the problems are not new. Consider the following quotation.

> On the personality and skill of (those staff in immediate charge of the children) depends primarily the happiness of the children in their care. ..... But such workers are too few to handle the work to be done, and some of them have had too little preparation for a very difficult task. ... This task has not been regarded as one calling for any special skill, and many of the children have suffered in consequence.

These are not the writings of Norman Warner or Sir William Utting but of Dame Myra Curtis in 1946. No doubt they were read with interest by Leila Rendel as she gathered around her motley groups of committed workers. The observations of Curtis were as relevant 20 years later when James King, faced with the retirement of Caldecott's ageing staff group, developed new structures to recruit and support residential workers. The arrival of Michael Jinks from the Cotswold Community in 1980 intensified the psychotherapeutic dimension of Caldecott's work and consequently asked more of the group workers.

To gather some insight into the staff world, we supplemented our intensive work within the eight living units and school that make up the Caldecott Community with a survey of all 170 working on the various sites on a selected day. This includes care workers, teachers, domestic and clerical staff and managers as well as several people who were not receiving a wage. The facts and figures emerging from this exercise will excite little surprise. The youth of the care workers (most are in their late teens or early twenties), the fact that three-quarters are women and that only a handful came from a minority ethnic group: - all of this is well known to those managing residential care. What we can do is to put some of this information into context and consider its implications for those providing a therapeutic environment for damaged children.

Since the Second World War, considerable efforts have been made nationally to provide training for residential staff but with limited success. Warner found that half of heads of homes had some suitable qualification for the post, but that four-fifths of other care staff were considered to have no relevant qualification at all, though the voluntary sector contained higher proportions of trained workers than the private or public sectors. This situation has changed very little since the 1960s. The Community would obviously prefer to employ trained workers, but there are simply not enough applications to restrict recruitment to those directly qualified. Instead it seeks to appoint care staff who:

- possess, at a minimum, basic literacy and numeracy skills and a "reasonable intellectual ability"
- ideally, have skills in artistic and leisure activities
- have some experience of working with children
- possess the capability for self-reflection and self-evaluation, particularly with regard to their own childhood
- are capable of *acquiring* therapeutic skills during their employment, through experience, training and supervision
- can meet the demands of team working and anti-sexist and anti-racist practice, and are appropriate role models for children.

This policy has allowed Caldecott to assemble a staff group that, whilst rarely specifically trained, is well educated and highly motivated. So, although few applicants have residential qualifications, more than three-quarters have benefited from further education, mostly at degree level. A common academic background is that of social work or sociology, but others have qualifications in health, mental health, education and various commercial subjects.

Given the youth and lack of direct qualifications of staff, training and development are accorded high priority. During the research period improvements in training were achieved, initially through the development of a Therapeutic Child Care Certificate. This consists of 180 hours of classroom time, 120 hours of reading, 30 hours of supervision and 30 hours of written work and has been running at the Community for the past five years. All residential and teaching staff are enrolled after a six month induction at the Community, and 27 are currently participating. Teaching is performed by senior staff, together with several outside consultants, and supervision is conducted fortnightly by team managers. The success of the programme encouraged the Community to open the Caldecott College which aims to be a nationally recognised centre of excellence in the training and development of residential social workers.

The setting

Had we been undertaking this study prior to the Second World War, we would have found a far higher proportion of staff living in the Community. Commentators have referred to a 'flight from residence' by children but the metaphor can also be applied to staff.

At the time of Curtis, nearly all staff were resident and when the Williams Committee reported in 1967 this proportion was still four-fifths. By the 1970s the proportion living in was about two-thirds but today it is unusual, outside the private sector, for a staff member to live in the same building as the children. Caldecott is unusual in that it offers accommodation to its staff but even those who live in the Community are situated at some distance from the children. Most care and teaching staff travel several miles to their workplace, and some commute long distances: a handful came in each day from London, 60 miles away. Most domestic, clerical and maintenance staff, by contrast, live much closer to their work.

The Caldecott approach represents a balance between old and new. To find the right calibre of staff it recruits from a wide geographical area. The offer of inexpensive accommodation helps to preserve a sense of community, while at the same time providing a sense of privacy for staff and the opportunity to switch-off from the considerable demands of the job. Caldecott's rural setting is not to the liking of all staff. Not everybody is attracted by open fields and muddy lanes: many do not wish to break their city ties. Only one in eight of the care teaching staff were attracted to Caldecott by its location although team managers were more favourable in their views. Nevertheless, the bulk of new staff are young college leavers who seldom have pre-existing housing commitments and greatly appreciate anything that bolsters their meagre income. Thus, few newly appointed care staff turn down Community housing, and some stay for many years.

The task

Those drawn to the work seem to find themselves involved in a range of tasks. However, much as contemporary care workers complain about the amount of cleaning and washing up they are obliged to do, they are considerably more fortunate than their forebears in this respect. Monsky in 1960 estimated that three-fifths of a residential worker's time was occupied by domestic chores. Today, at Caldecott, about 90 minutes of the fourteen hour working day is spent on such tasks and care workers have largely been relieved of administrative and domestic obligations. Clerical staff look after administration, the domestic staff look after cooking and cleaning while the maintenance staff see to the fabric of the building. The Jill of all trades housemother no longer exists and, as a consequence, the Community employs more than twice as many adults as it accommodates children.

The increasing specialisation of these staff has brought a touch of professionalism to mundane but important tasks such as mending clothes and repairing windows. It has also allowed the development of previously neglected roles such as staff training, semi-independence training and outreach work with older teenagers leaving the Community. As we have seen, Caldecott even employs "grandmothers" such as Kitty in Woodside to extend the range of experience from which children may benefit. Hence, another consequence of specialisation is an increasingly heterogeneous staff group, now ranging in age from teens to eighties, and with an equivalent range in terms of socio-economic, ethnic and personal backgrounds.

The transition from white, female, Christian staff groups familiar to

Leila Rendel to a staff complement more in tune with the Community's anti-discriminatory policies has not been without its tensions. For example, while Caldecott remains predominately a female establishment, men who remain in the job move quickly up the promotional ladder and thus exercise influence disproportionate to their numbers. Only two of the eight team managers are women, yet three-quarters of care and teaching staff are female.

The introduction of men into the Community and increased mingling of the sexes, both staff and children, has also raised the sexual temperature of the Community. The fundamental need to protect children does not always sit easily alongside workers' rights to be protected from unfair discrimination, disciplinary action or dismissal. Children separated from home demand intimacy with staff but it is impossible to ensure that contact between staff and children is always public and closely supervised. It would be pleasant to report that the Community had found a solution to this balancing act but, although recruitment, training and practice address such issues, pressures on Community staff are no less than in any other residential establishment.

Sensitivity to the cultural and spiritual experience of children has been a long-standing concern of the Community. The denominational concerns of the inter-war period have been largely superseded by issues of race and ethnicity but minority cultures at Caldecott are represented at present more by residents than by staff. The Community has made efforts, with some success, to recruit staff from ethnic minorities but more needs to be done. Some staff were concerned that children from ethnic minorities have their cultural needs neglected and many felt that more needed to be done in this area. Many worry that children from ethnic minorities might suffer from cultural isolation within the Community, and indeed some black staff had experienced this isolation themselves, both at Caldecott and in the local area.

Continuity

Clearly the Community invests heavily in its staff but does it help to achieve its aims for 'continuity and commitment from the grown ups?' Children's homes in the 1960s replaced a third of their staff every year, with half the leavers quitting the service altogether. However, a core of staff stayed on and two-thirds of housemothers surveyed by Williams had been in the service for five years or longer. This pattern of a small minority of long-stay staff at the top and frequent recruitment and resignation beneath has long been typical of residential care. Utting found that 45% of residential staff had been in post for less than two years although, the more optimist Warner estimated the average length of service to be 'around four years'.

The average length of service of care staff at Caldecott is around three and a half years. However, if we remove from the calculation managerial staff, most of whom had been in post for longer than eight years, the mean length of stay is reduced to two years. The bulk of experience at Caldecott is thus concentrated in its senior staff, with younger staff arriving and leaving fairly frequently.

This high turnover must be a concern to the Community. We found that nearly a quarter (23%) of its care staff departed in the last year of our research. This translates to an annual care staff turnover of 35 to 40%, much the same as identified by Williams 30 years ago. Care workers are nearly three times as likely to leave as other staff, and twice as likely to leave as teaching staff. Most of the care staff we talked to planned to stay less than two years and only a few saw their long term future at Caldecott. As in other residential contexts, continuity for children at Caldecott is more likely to be provided by domestic, maintenance, managerial and teaching staff than by care workers.

One consequence of this coming and going is a constant need to fill vacant posts and maintain staff complements. Given that Caldecott rarely employs relief or agency staff, a single unfilled vacancy requires each remaining staff member to work at least seven extra staff-hours, on top of a long working week. Whether this is achieved by actually working longer hours or by reducing staff cover, the consequences in terms of staff exhaustion are much the same. Care staff also have to cover for absences caused by sickness, holidays and training and for days off by domestic staff. The physical and emotional strain on those who remain in place is considerable and, as Siobhan's diary entries have shown, the throughput of staff is also felt by the children.

Additional strain is caused by the volume of new staff finding their way into the institution. Caldecott does not operate a formal induction programme and many staff felt ill prepared to start work and rather frightened by their sudden immersion into the hothouse. Some of the living units do make considerable efforts to integrate new staff but when existing staff are stretched, new staff are soon asked to 'pull their weight'. The care staff we talked to were unanimous in calling for better induction. Some felt that a period of 'shadowing' would be sufficient, others that a printed guidebook of maps, personnel and regulations would be a useful start, whilst some felt that only formal training prior to commencement of the job would be adequate.

Many of these difficulties are secondary to the problem of high turnover. How can this be tackled? The question has received considerable scrutiny in the post war period, not the least because it represents probably the single most significant barrier to the creation of an adequately trained workforce for the residential sector. The Community depends on a low cost, highly motivated and reasonably educated workforce for its survival; it allows management to be strong and keeps the fee charged to local authorities at a reasonable level. It is noticeable that there are no staff unions at Caldecott, a feature that marks it apart from local authority homes. Nonetheless, grumbles frequently heard from staff in other residential establishments were rarely expressed during the time researchers were at the Community. Staff do not appear particularly dissatisfied. Few felt unequal to the demands of the work and those who did expressed confidence that gaps could be remedied either by training or experience. Whilst long hours were a cause of complaint, staff did not particularly feel that their time was wasted in activities irrelevant to the children's welfare. All felt that they had opportunity to influence practice both through formal channels such as meetings and informally through innovation, leadership and example.

More could be done by changing the way in which candidates view residential work. Most care staff see Caldecott as a stepping stone to something else, an interesting interlude until that 'something' comes along, or a lifestyle experiment, rather than as a career in itself. Only a small minority see their long term future within residential child care. This is not to suggest that the staff were not on the whole committed to the caring professions - the majority intended to remain within the field of teaching, psychotherapy or social work with children and families. Few, however, saw their future within *residential* work.

That the job itself considerably accelerates the rate of turnover however is equally undeniable. Whilst no specific information was gathered on this question, staff left little doubt as to what *they* saw as the causes of high turnover:

> People are drained, overwhelmed and eventually they leave. You need to look at the pain. Residential social workers get hurt every day, physically and emotionally ... Many don't survive two years due in part to the Community's 'cannon fodder' attitude to them. Sometimes I feel like an NCO at Ypres. I just lead them over the top to slaughter.

Explanations for the lack of continuity must be sought in the demands of commitment, as the following description of daily tasks illustrates.

Conclusions

Many pages of doom and gloom have been devoted to the problems of staffing in residential care. The continuity of difficulties chronicled by Curtis, Williams, Levy and Kahan, Utting, Warner and many others is indeed depressing. But there is also a certain vitality in places like Caldecott. As staff make up two-thirds of the Community they are key to its mood and to any success it might achieve with children.

At the core, there is a group of senior managers (mainly men) and domestic staff who have long worked at the Community. Around this are gathered a group of young, educated and highly motivated people who come from outside Ashford and have yet to decide on their future life plans. They are committed to helping people but not necessarily in a residential context. Caldecott's efforts to train these new recruits in the therapeutic method are admirable but levels of support in the first few weeks are clearly insufficient. Nonetheless, relying much on the model developed by James King 30 years ago, a viable social system has evolved and while, like any organisation, Caldecott suffers periods of difficulty and crisis, generally speaking, like house doctors in hospitals, staff are happy but are extremely tired, bordering on exhaustion.

A day in the life of Caldecott staff

For care staff at Caldecott, commitment is not an optional extra. One young group worker eloquently summarised her experience as follows:

> The lengthy hours can be explained but until you've worked them and watched any personal life disintegrate it's difficult to really

understand. This really is a lifestyle, not a job. The closest I can get to giving an applicant some insight would be to set up an interview where one person made them feel worthless, disliked, scorned, skill-less, inadequate, sad, confused and overwhelmed and another would build them up and make them feel special, valued, appreciated, insightful, perceptive, trusted and honoured. Because that is what the kids do to us day in day out as well as the adult dynamic. This is what leaves us so drained. Normal social activities, personal relationships, *et cetera* conflict with the expectation of commitment. One or the other has to give.

The child care staff endure these pressures over very long shifts. In fact, because the needs of children do not respect shifts, most staff remain on campus for considerable periods in addition to their ordinary weekly routine. In the seven days prior to our survey, the care staff had worked an average of 75 hours. This was usually composed of five fourteen-hour days (from eight in the morning to ten at night) with a turn at being the person to sleep in the unit overnight. The newly built units are designed to have two members of staff sleeping-in, thus increasing the load. But some had done more. Those returning from a camping trip for older children had managed only a few hours off during the previous five days and their weekly total of hours ran into three figures. Eight weeks holiday a year seems small recompense for such efforts.

The main burden of time spent with children falls to the care staff. Team managers and their assistants work similar hours, but with greater variation over the term. When a team is at full strength, managers can adopt a more hands-off approach, even working a nine to five day. When a team falls below full strength however, or when other problems arise, it is often the managers who are expected to step into the breach, and thus effectively do two jobs at once.

Teaching staff too work long hours in term time, but no longer than their colleagues in public sector ordinary or special schools. The hours of clerical, domestic, maintenance and managerial staff are likewise essentially comparable to their counterparts in other organisations. By contrast, care workers in the public sector work 39 hours a week, and unions in local government are currently asking for this to be reduced to 37 hours. Caldecott care staff have a working week almost twice as long as that of their public sector colleagues.

Table 7: A day in the life of a residential social worker at Caldecott

Time	Activity	Hrs/Day
Before school	Leave home, Travel to Caldecott. Read messages from previous day. Handover procedures from sleep-in staff.	1.5
	Communicate with school. Help/supervise children waking, washing, dressing. Breakfast with children. Supervise/help children tidy bedrooms, clean teeth, brush hair, etc. Walk children to school. Hand over to school staff.	2.0
Morning school	Domestic duties, shopping, getting to and from school. Looking after children not in school. Visits to dentist, etc.	Variable
	Communication and meetings with parents and outside professionals.	0.5
	Training, supervision and internal meetings.	1.0
	Paperwork and administration.	0.5
	Chatting, drinking coffee, reading paper, etc.	1.0
Lunch	Collect children from school. Eat lunch with children. Occupy children until afternoon school. Return children to school.	2.0
Afternoon	As morning school. Prepare drink/snack for after school.	0.5
After school	Pick up children from school. Drink and snack. Supervise play or organise activities. Cook and eat tea. Wash up. Take children to outside activity. Supervise/organise children until bedtime and getting ready for bed. Spend twenty minutes with 'key' children, reading story, playing games etc. Lights out.	5.0
After lights out	Clear up debris. Prepare for morning: ironing clothes, laying breakfast table, etc. Write up day books. Any unfinished tasks from the day - reports, phone calls, discussions, etc. Travel home.	1.0
22.3	End of day	
	Total	**15.0**
	Free time	1.0

Not all of this time is spent in direct contact with children but even whilst the children are at school there is no shortage of necessary jobs to be done. When everything runs according to plan, the life of a Caldecott group worker would looks something like the timetable on the facing page. If, however, we add the inevitable crises of work with vulnerable children we can begin to understand the stress with which care workers cope. Siobhan has already told us how she swallowed glass, sat on the balcony ledge outside her bedroom window and had to be rescued after hanging by her fingertips from a motorway bridge. We asked staff to re-count other incidents which they had experienced in the year prior to the survey. The following two are typical:

> In the midst of a bad week we had two boys off school for mis-behaviour. Their acting out - smashing windows, climbing on roof, running off - continued until the manager broke down in tears and left mid-shift. The boys were only contained sometime after midnight.

> I was attacked by a child unprovoked whilst I was on my own in the group. He threw knives at me, smashed a window to get me, threw four chairs at me and then he tried to attack me with a huge pole with a metal end.

Such incidents are rare but it is their very unpredictability, the sudden crystallisation of a potentially life-threatening situation out of an apparently trivial incident, which tightens the screw of tension. As one care worker said, 'long hours accompanied by the intensity and high levels of stress can be detrimental to one's health'. Commitment thus takes many forms. The sheer length of the working day; the provocation withstood and failures endured; and the willingness to sacrifice personal time to deal with crises demand unswerving loyalty to the Community.

Most staff do all of this willingly, confident in the belief that Caldecott represents the children's best chance of overcoming their difficulties. On the other hand, care workers, teachers and domestic staff are not purely philanthropists: by their own account, they draw a variety of rewards from their lifestyles. Chief amongst these is the personal satisfaction gained from the progress of their charges, and the sense of self-worth which comes from confronting and overcoming challenges that have defeated previous carers and schools. Such positive experiences of working at the Community included:

> Watching kids gain control of their lives and move on to where they want to be .... also, equally, recognising that I did cope with (a very difficult situation) and learnt to deal with the pressure and intensity.

> Working with a Unit who were so demoralised and debilitated by an extremely troubled/damaged ten year old who resorted to knives and chairs as an attack at least two or three times a day ..... supporting the team to the extent that they were able to hold the child and now see the success they are having with him. It is wonderful.

Others draw on the more tangible rewards of experience and training upon which future careers in social work or psychotherapy can be built. Staff also acknowledge the attractiveness of the physical and social environment, and fringe benefits such as the offer of accommodation. Ultimately, however, the reward seems to come from "just being part of it really - the pride and love for our children, the sense of real commitment". Commitment, for many staff, is its own reward.

Conclusion

Caldecott's demands for 'continuity and commitment from the grown-ups' are frequently incompatible. Few staff have either the determination or the lack of alternatives to endure the pressures of the job indefinitely. The patterns we have described in this chapter are not untypical of the voluntary sector, in which costs to purchasers are maintained at artificially low levels by reliance on the dedication and commitment of young, idealistic staff who are prepared to take on a difficult job. Staff are enabled to operate in these conditions only by their belief in the efficacy and moral necessity of what they are doing, and even then only for a short period if not promoted to a more supervisory role. Such belief is not a particularly conspicuous feature of residential care at the moment, but it is difficult to see how the Community could continue to function without it.

Caldecott remains in some ways a pioneer. In its refusal to wait for national bodies to develop an adequate system of qualifications before mounting major initiatives in training, for example, it reaffirms the role of the voluntary sector as innovator. In other ways, staffing at the Community reflects changes in value systems, labour markets and management styles that have affected all residential establishments over the post-war period. Fundamentally, however, staffing remains cast in a traditional mould. The Community itself is somewhat proud of its commitment to the 'core values' of residential care, though its demands on staff are probably as much a matter of economic necessity as of deliberate policy. The problems associated with these core values are clear from the preceding pages. However, we must also report that public sector attempts to combat weaknesses in this approach by the diversion of ever more resources to staff have not notably reduced wastage or created a trained and experienced workforce. For all the deficiencies of Caldecott's approach, few others have found viable alternatives.

The children's view of the staff

During her stay, Siobhan conducted a survey among children in Woodside canvassing their views on the adults. In many respects this can be treated as an aside to the main business of understanding the Caldecott Community and measuring its effectiveness. Certainly, the winners and losers in Siobhan's poll are incidental to the principal tasks of this study. In other respects, however, Siobhan's work gives us important insights into the residential world. The questions give a clue to which personal attributes of staff are of interest to children; how attractive they are, whether they moan and groan and how they dress. The emphasis on time-keeping is revealing and the amount of time going from point to point is reflected in the questions about driving ability.

The survey indicates that staff are closely scrutinised by children; and children are ruthless judges. Moreover, while a supervisor, researcher or quality assessor may report results sensitively, children can be blunt. After this exercise, Derek, the most qualified of the staff members, was told 'You're the worst on time, the most unreliable and the least fashionable'. The hapless Derek was also to discover that he was the least outgoing, practically a crime in a residential context! As later sections demonstrate, children's views of staff (especially the young and vulnerable staff) are as draining on their morale as the long hours and other demands of working in a residential context with the troubled and troublesome.

Table 8: Siobhan's staff survey

	1st	Number of kids	2nd	Number of kids
Prettiest	Kate	6	Kathy	4
Softest	Tristan	4	Vick/Derek	2
Moaniest	Stella	8	Kirstie/Zoe	1
Kindest	Vic	4	Joanne	2
Funniest	Tristan	5	Ben	4
Fashionable	Ben	4	Kirstie	3
Unfashionable	Derek	7	Vick/Jo/Stella	1
Handsomest	Tristan	9	Vick	1
Fairest	Tristan	5	Vick	2
Worst on time	Derek	10		
Best on time	Kathy/Ben	5		
Reliable	Tristan/Ben	5		
Unreliable	Derek	5	Vick/Stella	2
Happiest	Steve	3	Vick	2
Unhappiest	Norma/Ben	3	Kirstie	2
Outgoing	Tristan	10		
Unoutgoing	Derek	6	Norma/Vick	1
Best driver	Kathy	4	Vick/Tristan	3

"

Siobhan and the outside world

When we last saw Siobhan, she had made a decision to call herself Yates rather than Kelly. This change did not endure but in many other respects Siobhan's life did shift after this point. The mood in the diaries alters. There is far more about other people in the group and in the world beyond Caldecott than about Siobhan. The record is of progress with intermittent crises and it is this that we try to capture in the coming pages.

The first major development was the conclusion of the first stage of the disclosure process, 22 months after arriving at the Community. It was marked by a meeting between social services, police, Caldecott staff and Siobhan at which the police constable told her:

- He believed everything Siobhan had said.
- He had discussed the situation with colleagues and they had come to the conclusion that taking further statements from Siobhan's family would be unhelpful.
- Statements were to remain on the child protection team's file.
- Following a review, Siobhan and her brother Nigel were to meet to resolve their difficulties.
- Supervised contact with her brother Wayne was to begin.
- Supervised contact with mother could start when and if Siobhan was ready.

Relatively little attention was given to the maltreatment Siobhan suffered. Apart from a handful of visits to Doctor Hirshi and the open offer to see the Community psychiatrist Doctor Earle or psychologist Philip Maggs, questions of abuse diminished. Whether or not this strategy was in Siobhan's best interests, only time will tell. We do know that the lack of a full follow-up after disclosure was a feature of Siobhan's decision to leave Caldecott, as later sections will illustrate. Nonetheless, fewer concerns about abuse did mean progress in other areas. The setbacks were just as dangerous (and potentially harmful) as before but they were less frequent. An overdose of paracetamol, being attacked by a man while absconding and other less vivid breakdowns emerge in the following pages. Steps forward and back can largely be attributed to three aspects of Siobhan's life; her education, the group in which she lived and her contacts with relations.

Education

After the disclosure, the most significant change in Siobhan's circumstances at Caldecott, and probably the most important to her long term life chances, was securing a place at the local Grammar school, known as Highworth. The Community puts great emphasis on education and, whenever possible, encourages children into mainstream schools. Many achieve well but few get the opportunity to attend a Grammar school and Siobhan was the first to make this transition in many years.

The entrance procedure was stringent: an exam followed by interviews with nine teachers. We have described elsewhere the difficulties looked after children experience when they have to re-integrate into mainstream schools. It says much for Siobhan's resilience that she was able to overcome these obstacles and begin her classes with relative ease. The sense of achievement was not lost on her as on the 12th of March, in the middle of a mundane list of doctor's visits, group meetings and a visit from the researcher she writes...

I'VE PASSED!!!!

I couldn't believe it.

The change in school had considerable effects upon Siobhan. Naturally it raised her self esteem. Not one of the 250 strong Community failed to hear about her triumph and, risking a Hawthorne effect, neither could the researchers hide their delight. But in the long run the chief impact has come from the exhausting routine of Grammar school work, the endless homework, the rigour of time spent in class, the social activities and school trips. Even the journey to and from school added an hour to her school day. Siobhan was faced with considerable demands from outside the Community and this affected - mostly for the better - her behaviour within Caldecott.

It was a difficult transition to manage. Moving to Highworth meant leaving the Caldecott school. In the Community classes Siobhan was the outstanding pupil while in the Grammar school she initially aspired to be average. In interviews with the research team, she eloquently described her social changes, the friends missed, the initial sense of loneliness in the large new school and the feeling of being the odd one out, even among the many Caldecott children who travelled into Ashford and other towns for mainstream education.

8th of April

> At bedtime Kate came to speak to me. I've been feeling a bit upset lately because now I am at Highworth I don't hardly ever see Donna or Peter and other people who are important to me. Kate said she'll make sure that there is time for me to see them and she will try to spend more time with me after school. I felt much better afterwards. Went to sleep almost straight away!

It is partly a measure of the tolerance and support of the mainstream school that Siobhan endured these pressures. She quickly integrated and, whilst she was the only looked after child and the only one travelling from a residential centre, she was not made to feel different. The ethos of the school was clearly reflected in the kindness displayed by Siobhan's fellow pupils. The school remained tolerant throughout Siobhan's subsequent breakdowns and admitted her back after absences sometimes consequent upon her own misbehaviour.

Progress at Highworth can also be attributed to Caldecott's efforts in preparing Siobhan for the move and supporting her thereafter. Their efforts were exemplary. The expectation and encouragement attached to homework, the high status afforded to educational pursuits and the availability of specialist staff to help with particular problems made the difference between Siobhan succeeding and failing at Highworth. The diary entries regularly record days at school, followed by homework after tea and evening trips to the Caldecott school for help with Maths or English or Geography. Whole Sundays devoted to homework were not unusual and with several libraries and other quiet places to choose from, Siobhan was clearly well placed.

There is much of practical value that other residential centres could learn from Caldecott's efforts with education. The employment of staff who have themselves succeeded educationally undoubtedly helps but is not essential. It is the learning environment that counts and the expectations placed upon children to perform to their best ability and to improve. As we write this, Siobhan is just celebrating her 16th birthday. In five years time, in ten years, her situation is as likely to reflect Caldecott's efforts in the area of education as in any other part of her life. Yet in other residential centres education remains a low priority and had Siobhan been placed in a local authority setting like her brother Nigel, we would have not have been surprised if she had received no classes at all.

There were also immediate rewards. After just three months at Highworth Siobhan writes in her diary:

26th of June

> Had another good day in school. I'm glad I am doing well in school. It's the longest I've ever stayed in a school without having a bad reputation and I hope that it stays that way....

The mood of the group

As Siobhan completed the first step in understanding her experiences of abuse and took her place in the Grammar school, she slowly but surely became marginal within Woodside. As much as anything, this change can be attributed to the length of Siobhan's stay. Eighteen months after

Siobahn's arrival, Mandy and Hayley departed and Siobhan became, at 14, one of the senior members of the group, an old hand. Departures of long-standing staff which caused so much distress in the early part of her story were later recorded almost routinely. For example,

14th of July

> We had a group meeting and Ben announced that he was leaving
> the group next Tuesday. I wasn't surprised.

We have described the way in which a group can change. Woodside was one of the most stable parts of the Community but it too was subject to difficult periods. The arrival of a young but violent girl put considerable stress upon adults and children alike. By December of the year Siobhan transferred to Highworth, staff departures and illness combined with children's difficult behaviour brought the unit to its knees. Siobhan's diary entry clearly captures the gravity of the situation.

1st of December

> Had a good day in school. Had older/younger meetings today.
> The researcher phoned. Kate went home at teatime and gradu-
> ally the evening got worse. Nearly the whole group started. We
> had a group meeting loads of people had to be held during it. I
> just sat and cried. I can't believe how much the group has changed.
> For a very long time Woodside has been the most settled group
> in the Community, there were very few problems (once I came
> through all my problems). We done a lot of things together and
> actually respected and cared for each other like a family. We nearly
> always stuck together in everything we done. Now it seems that
> everything is lost, no children care about each other anymore.
> The level of violence has increased dramatically. I mean tonight
> there was so many adults who were punched, kicked, bitten and
> spat at in the face. It makes me really upset. It did calm down
> later though. Done my homework really late.

2nd of December

> Well I got back from a nice day in school to find Woodside in a
> right old mess. Apparently at lunchtime the whole group apart
> from me and two others went. The group was being loud so Stella
> called everyone together. During the meeting Tina was shouting
> and swearing (she had been mucking around all morning). Matt

tookTina by the hand and was about to takeTina out of the room. Tina shouted 'HELP'.Tony shouted 'Let's get them'. All seven children got up and attacked the adults very badly.Then Tony and (a recent arrival) Emma ran away. I caught them just by luck when I got back and everyone was being held. It was so horrible.We had a three hour group meeting. No one has resolved anything, they are all acting stupid still not accepting anything.A lot of adults have been very badly hurt. Kate had to come in on her day off. I really can't believeTony andTina, two of the oldest doing that and all the others joining in. I am very upset by all this.Went to bed late. I didn't manage to do my homework.

Unfortunately this description would be familiar to many children in residential homes in England andWales. From Siobhan's writings, we can comprehend why so many homes close in crisis and see the consequences of marginally increased pressure upon staff and children. Even the worldly wise Siobhan failed to get her homework done on the night of the 2nd of December.The breakdown in Woodside was temporary and was overcome by the Community's ability to call in resources from elsewhere on the campus. Had the unit been isolated within a local authority management structure, it almost certainly would have closed.

Thus, with time, Siobhan's commitment toWoodside waned. Group meetings seldom focused upon the successful, unproblematic child and they became incidental to Siobhan. Group meetings were for 'other people's problems' and they were frequently described as 'boring'. Her contemporaries Hayley and Mandy left, to be replaced by younger children at the same stage of development as Siobhan when she came to Caldecott. A sense of *déja vu*, the idea that some people had moved on leaving Siobhan behind and the failure to resolve all of the problems linked to the abuse contributed to her growing disillusionment. In the end she decided to leave.As with the disclosure, she told her diary first.

2nd of November
> This may come as a shock to you, but I am seriously considering leaving Woodside for a number of reasons:
> I am bored.
> There is no one here of my age and interests.
> The little ones irritate me.
> I don't get hardly any attention.
> I haven't talked about my problems for ages.

I can't see myself growing or moving forward from this point.
I am always depressed.
I feel isolated from the world.
I don't get enough freedom.
I need to be around more people of my age.
Anyway, these are some of the issues around me at the moment, and more besides.

Family relationships

Maybe the 'more besides' referred to home. References in the diary to relatives decreased during Siobhan's stay at Caldecott. The principal link was with brother Nigel with whom Siobhan was removed from home. This contact largely consisted of telephone calls – many of which ended unsatisfactorily – and a few visits. There were no letters (although Siobhan is a prolific and articulate writer) and lists of people to send Christmas cards and holiday postcards to or of presents received at birthdays are notable for the absence of family members. Anniversaries of previous visits are noted, such as 'it's a year since I last saw mum' or 'it's two years since I talked to Barry'. By the standards of modern child care, by what we know from contemporary research or by the expectations of the *Children Act*, 1989, contact and other access arrangements were unsatisfactory.

It might be said that this is an unusual case: it was necessary that Siobhan's father and eldest brother should have access stopped, for she needed to be protected from these people. Indeed, there were times during Siobhan's stay at Caldecott when she was fearful of her father who periodically would try to find out where she lived and try to get in touch. We have not under-estimated the distress caused by these situations.

However, in the context of children looked after by the state – or even of children whose names have been placed on the Child Protection Register – Siobhan's situation is not unusual. In the long term, family relationships are likely to be important to her, as they are important to nearly all readers of this book. When a child is looked after by a local authority, the law expects that, unless they are clearly harmful, visits, telephone calls, letters and exchanges of photographs and greetings cards will be encouraged and carefully managed. As we shall see, parents are frightened by places like Caldecott and children do not necessarily know how to handle telephone calls. Left to their own devices, parents and other relatives gradually lose touch with children looked after by local authorities.

The principal features of Siobhan's access arrangements were, first, the infrequency of visits, second, that it was largely due to Siobhan's persistence that links were kept alive at all and, third, that, almost without exception, contact took place away from Caldecott. It was Siobhan telephoning, Siobhan visiting and Siobhan holding her hand out to relatives and friends that kept her in touch with them. None of the researchers visiting Caldecott ever left with a sense that families were welcome or were wanted at the Community.

At certain moments of crisis, however, families became important. We will see later that many children departing the Community in an unplanned way return to relatives - and nearly all children in the long term go home. When Siobhan swallowed 30 paracetamols, it was to family that hospital and Community staff turned. The overdose precipitated contact with mum and brother Adrian which had been neglected for over twelve months.

15th of June

> Today was awful. I didn't go to school. In the afternoon I took an overdose of 30 paracetamols. I was taken to hospital in an ambulance. Kirstie came with me. I was put on a drip. Kate and Richard stayed with me until 1.45 am. I was put on a drip and had loads of needles. I was given some medicine which made me sick. Only too sick. I don't remember anything that happened.

16th of June

> Today I found out what really happened yesterday. I went from stages of being conscious and unconscious many times, I had conversations and said some weird things which I cannot remember. I was violently sick for intervals of six or seven minutes. I had a very high level of paracetamol in my blood and needed a drip with a very high pressure, in order to neutralise my blood. Kate and Richard were really worried about me. I feel really bad for putting them through that. Well today I saw a psychiatrist and poured out all my problems to her, knowing I'll never see her again so I don't need to worry. When Kate came to see me in the

evening, I phoned up my mum with her for the first time in over a year. Lots of people came to see me today. I had lots of cards and flowers and things, which has made me feel even more guilty than I was feeling already. This is the most selfish thing I have ever done in my whole life. My drip came off late tonight. I still feel very ill.

Unfortunately having resurrected contact with her mother, Caldecott did not sustain the momentum, a failure that had predictable results. Siobhan's disclosure mostly took place without her mother's participation and against the backdrop of mother's denials. At some point – whether during Siobhan's stay at Caldecott or afterwards – the disagreement had to be resolved. But as the following quotation illustrates, frustrations were allowed to accumulate and eventually spill over during a row that began as a petty dispute.

Well Nigel phoned me yesterday evening (21st of October) and he asked me to phone mum and to get her to phone him. I did it but it went seriously wrong. She started it by making me feel bad about something. Then I just got everything off my chest. I told her things I never thought I'd hear myself saying. I brought up stuff about the past and what she'd done and she denied everything again. Because of my frustration I ended up crying and screaming and shouting at her. I told her I didn't want anything to do with her again. Even if she admitted to things, I hate her so much and as far as I am concerned she can stay out of my life for good. That way I'll be a lot happier.

Conclusion

Following Siobhan's disclosure of sexual abuse, the principal focus of Caldecott's work switched to her education. The rewards of this investment become manifest later in the study and should stand Siobhan in good stead for many years. In other respects the Community contributed to her recovery, not least through the stability and security offered by Woodside and through the perseverance of staff facing up to her misbehaviour. We have also identified weaknesses in their approach, and some of Siobhan's problems remain unresolved at the time of writing. The routine of life in Woodside also took its toll on Siobhan's commitment and belief in the Community. As we leave her in this section she is determined to leave, much against the wishes of her social worker and the adults in Woodside. We shall pick up her story again shortly.

Outside looking in

To conclude this part of the book, we consider the views of those supporting the child outside the Community: the children's parents, other relatives and professionals such as social workers and education specialists who secured a place at Caldecott in the first instance. Their role in Caldecott's life should not be under estimated. After all, unlike Siobahn, many of the children should enjoy regular contact with relatives. We have described the treatment programme and the practicalities of implementing this but social workers will also exert considerable influence on plans for the child, not least in deciding the length of stay and mode of departure.

When we began the study, we were expecting to find difficulties in the ability of residential and field social workers to liaise, share tasks and communicate effectively. This is a common problem in residential care. We have expressed our reservations about the quality of family links for children at Caldecott. Much of the evidence we collected confirmed that we were right to have these concerns. Indeed, our explanations showed that, while life within the Community can be very rosy, problems outside - and in the child's home - continue.

We gathered evidence by interviewing the relatives of the children living in Woodside with Siobhan. We also talked to social workers and other professionals supporting these children. We deal with their perspectives separately, first the parents then the professionals. We provide a case study of the conflicts that can arise when the views of those outside Caldecott fail to coincide with those inside. This concerns Thomas Bozzi whose departure from Caldecott was nothing short of disastrous.

Parents' perspectives

Parents are frightened by Caldecott. As if it was a National Trust home, they tiptoe around the house privately trying to work out what kind of place it is. Their children are the ornaments, not to be touched. There is a cultural gap between the parents and the Community which is difficult to bridge. The books, the pictures, the 'pedimented Tuscan doorcase,' as it is described in 'Pevsner', the marble chimney pieces and plaster ceilings represent a different world for many parents.

In this context they must watch while somebody else brings up 'their baby'. Not surprisingly, there are tensions, many of which come to a head over apparently trivial issues. Mrs Bozzi, for example, was violated by the Community allowing Thomas to wear an earring. 'Only women in my family wear earrings', she said, 'No male in my household is going to wear an earring'. This clash of cultural expectations was common.

Such difficulty is exacerbated by the simple barriers of distance and routine which stand between parents and their children. Tina Richmond's mother needed travel vouchers to pay for the train from Birmingham, where she lived, to Ashford. Getting to the social services office was itself something of a problem, getting from Birmingham to Ashford was a nightmare. As there was nowhere for her to stay at Caldecott and the 200 mile round trip had to be managed in a day, the visit itself seldom lasted longer than two hours. Exhausted by the journey, Mrs Richmond always felt ill-prepared for seeing her daughter and left, rather disenchanted, to reflect on her failure as a mother during the four hours it took to get back home.

Not every parent has such a long journey but most find the trip to Caldecott difficult to organise. When they arrive, they quickly find themselves without a role. Several parents described themselves as being piggy-in-the-middle, caught between their children 'at home' in Caldecott and the staff acting *in loco parentis*. A few parents referred to the 'brainwashing' of their offspring when staff encouraged the children to behave in a particular way during visits. Siobhan's mother used the phrase 'staff watching' meaning that her daughter constantly looked to Kate and Stella for approval during visiting times. Mrs Kelly, like all the parents and other relations we talked to, felt very uncomfortable among a group of children and staff and resented the limited opportunities for privacy afforded by the Woodside regime.

If contacts between parents and children were more regular, many of these problems could be ironed out. But we found contact to be spasmodic, a pattern which added to the tension of the meetings when they did occur. As Mrs Clarke, Kevin and Neil's mother, explained:

I don't like going to Caldecott but I want to see my boys. So I make the arrangements and I worry about it for weeks. I'm angry at the staff and I think about what I'm going to say to them and then I think about the boys and making it nice for them. In the end I'm in a lather worrying about it and the visit takes place and I leave the boys to go back to Woodside and I walk away feeling empty. I hate it. I'm sure they hate it. But I've got to keep going, after all that's said and done, they are my boys, it's to me that they belong.

Much of Mrs Clarke's interaction with Caldecott involves the young group workers we described earlier. Many members of staff consider parents ill-informed about children's needs and many, rightly perhaps, are angry about what parents have done or have allowed to happen to their children. However group workers perceive the situation, most parents know more about their child than anybody else. Parents also know how their children are feeling, if only because many had much the same experiences when they were young. They have failed their children just as they were failed by their own parents. Unfortunately, parents often carry the deep wounds of having neglected or abused their children and the strictures of young group workers add salt to these wounds.

Between visits and other contacts with their children, life must continue for the parents. They leave abusing partners and meet new ones. They have more children or welcome them back from other substitute care settings. They battle with their problems. Mrs Clarke undertook personal counselling, Mrs Adams fought to get a bigger house and Mrs Richmond tackled her social worker to maintain her child's knowledge about her ethnic origins. All of this took place without Caldecott's knowledge.

If the Community hopes to improve the circumstances of the children it shelters, it will have to work with the family, gain insight into the problems that the child faced at home and may have to face again in the future. This deficiency can make the difference between good and bad outcomes, as later sections will show.

Professional perspectives

Most social workers, educationalists, psychiatrists and psychologists associated with the children in Caldecott have some belief in the value of a therapeutic Community. Most of the professionals we talked to had been instrumental in getting the children to Caldecott in the first place, so they were highly likely to be complimentary about the approach. Like the staff at Caldecott, professionals focused on the child first and relatives second. In fact, many social workers admitted to reducing the time spent with family members since the child had been admitted to the Community.

The interviews with professionals were marked by a concern with the current situation of the child. As long as the child was secure and happy in the short term, professionals expressed high levels of satisfaction with the Community's work. We did not get any indication of long term plans or ideas about how Caldecott might complement other forms of support, such as making the parental home a viable place to which the child might return. The strategy which professionals adopt is, of course, entirely understandable. Caldecott takes a difficult case off their hands and another soon comes along to takes its place. It is a pattern of working, however, which may be detrimental to the long term interests of those children placed at Caldecott.

Professional concern is most evident during difficult moments of transition. The policy of moving older children from the main campus to the unit at Lacton Hall devoted to adolescents, for example, causes anxiety in the other units. As we shall see, it was a factor in Siobhan's decision to leave the Community. Nearly all of the outside professionals we talked to picked up this tension. It was not that they had a firm view about whether it was wise to move children around the campus, it was more that they had to respond to concerns being expressed by relatives and children about the stability of the placement. The mood is captured well by Mandy Atkinson's social worker

> I was quite happy with the Caldecott plan but the move to Lacton was a bit of a mess. Mandy didn't want to go plus her mother didn't find out until she phoned Woodside and Mandy had gone. I was up and down to Caldecott all the time at that period and it was all crisis management. I don't really know what the move was supposed to achieve and it was ultimately a disaster but even if it had been a necessity it was a transition badly handled, both by me and by them.

The relationship between the professional in the home community and the specialist that provides the care is prone to difficulty. Many of the professionals we spoke to observed that they were criticised both for being too distant from the Community and, on other occasions, for being too close, even meddlesome. In none of the cases we scrutinised was there an effective allocation of roles and responsibilities between outside professionals, family members, Caldecott staff and the child. In most instances, this led to little more than an underlying tension and a feeling of unease such as that described by Mandy Atkinson's social worker. When however there is a major crisis it can lead to feelings of bitterness and rejection which last long after the child's departure.

The following case study, concerning Thomas Bozzi, illustrates the problems that can arise. As the final sections of the book show, Thomas's departure from Caldecott was not typical but would have been seen as such by his parents, social workers and other professionals.

Case Study: Thomas Bozzi

As we described earlier, Thomas and his brother Tony were the sons of an African father and Caribbean mother. They had been physically abused by their father and suffered much disruption away from home. The brothers settled well and over the following years achieved a sense of security and stability unknown to them for some time. There were occasional minor blow-ups when the boys ran away but generally their stay was relatively tranquil.

As he got older, it was suggested that Thomas should leave Tony and Woodside and move on to the adolescent unit at Lacton Hall. Thomas began to behave aggressively, bullying the younger children in Woodside and in the Caldecott school. Already stretched by the behaviour of Emma, the violent girl described earlier, the Community suspended Thomas for two weeks and he was sent home. His social worker, Ursula Karakusovic and co-worker Sheila Mear were not informed or consulted about the exclusion and called a meeting with Community staff to review the placement. Unfortunately, owing to a communication error that meeting did not take place and after a series of frenetic and sometimes terse telephone calls, it was decided that Thomas should return to Caldecott for six weeks to round off the treatment plan before returning to his mother. The move to Lacton Hall was abandoned.

The change of plan served to upset Thomas further. Three days after returning to Woodside he got into an argument with the group worker who knew him best, threatening to hit him with a golf club. He was expelled from the Community that evening. All of his belongings were bundled together and, again without consultation with Ursula Karakusovic or Sheila Mear, Thomas was sent home. He was followed, a few weeks later, by Tony. The quotation gives an indication of the outsider's perceptions of the breakdown. These are themselves important as they influence children's long-term situation and also affect the way in which local authorities and parents view Caldecott. First the boys' mother, Mrs Bozzi.

Mrs Bozzi

I didn't know what was going on. First (Caldecott) didn't want anything to do with me, next they are saying you can have him back. We never did see eye to eye and then things went from bad to worse. When I got him back he was totally out of control. I needed more help then than I did before he went to Caldecott but the staff didn't want anything to do with him. They rejected him and they rejected me. Social services were not much better.

Ursula Karakusovic talking to her co-worker Sheila Mear

Ursula: It never really worked with Thomas. The staff see mother as really obstructive (which actually she is) but they have also been difficult with me.

Sheila: Was the ethnic background of the children a problem?

Ursula: I don't think they understood the importance of his cultural background but I wouldn't have said it was a problem. It was just steady deterioration in relationships. Appointments were missed and just before I left on maternity leave I wrote a letter of complaint to Caldecott only to get a snotty letter back from one of the team leaders. It was going downhill for a long time.

Sheila: Well whoever was to blame, the way it ended was a disgrace. I don't think anybody in this team would think about using Caldecott again. Or even a therapeutic community again.

Ursula: It was the rejection that we could not understand. And now we are left with a boy who is not bad enough for a secure unit (after all he did not actually attack the member of staff at Caldecott) but he is running riot at home and no foster home would have him.

We have described the unusual situation of a child being removed from the Community by Caldecott staff. It is an object lesson for residential social workers and field officers on the importance of effective communication and the consequences of poor liaison. None of the parties emerged with reputations unscathed by this episode but it is Thomas who has suffered, who has been rejected not only by his natural home but also by the place where he was sent for protection and support.

What should this liaison have consisted of? It was the absence of long term objectives and contingency plans that failed Thomas. Ursula Karakusovic and Sheila Mear used Caldecott to shelter the Bozzi children but neither had much idea about what should happen afterwards. The Community protected Thomas from physical attack and provided a warm, supportive environment, but effectively shut out the boys' mother. But once the boys were safe, what next? As a matter of routine, Lacton Hall was explored as a option and Thomas reacted to the insecurity of his position by testing the boundaries of the Community's tolerance. With no contingency plans to fall back on, Thomas's behaviour deteriorated, as did the relationship between Caldecott and the local authority. As we shall see in the next part of this study, the outcomes could hardly have been worse.

Conclusions

Caldecott is a community which the outside world finds hard to penetrate. It focuses inward on the children, seeking to provide a stable environment in which residents can develop emotionally and educationally. The Caldecott approach is underpinned by a treatment programme which is difficult to understand and is clouded in a mysterious nomenclature. It is easy in these circumstances for the world outside to be and feel excluded.

Had we been undertaking this study in the days of Leila Rendel, the precarious relationship between life in Caldecott and life outside would hardly have been a concern. Children were rescued from their parents or were volunteered to Caldecott's care and it was frequently accepted that professionals in the home community had also failed the child. Today the situation is different. It is well known that most children return to live with their parents or will use them as an important source of support. Indeed, the continuing importance of relatives in the child's life is now enshrined in legislation which refers to enduring parental responsibility even when the child has to live away from home. Social workers should oversee this process and are, in any case, vital to Caldecott's existence because they pay the fees that maintain the Community.

By our reckoning, many of the difficulties that surround the relationship of Caldecott to the outside world could be resolved with better planning. Concomitant to such a strategy would be a clear allocation of roles to tackle both the needs of the child and the family. At present it is possible for plans to run out of steam and for parents, outside professionals and Caldecott staff to lose confidence. Crises tend to crystallise in moments of transition such as moving from Caldecott to mainstream classes, or from the main campus to Lacton Hall, or when children move into puberty.

We know from previous research that only five per cent of all separated children manage to find enduring stability away from their relatives. Nearly all of these children are in foster or adoptive homes but Caldecott could be a viable alternative. Maybe one of the eight living units could be devoted to children whose contacts with home are negligible or have been severed. But for most, the continued involvement of relatives is likely to be important for children's long term well-being.

Part Five

Life after Caldecott

"

Engineering a departure

Siobhan decided she wanted to leave the Community well before members of staff knew about it. As is the case with many at Caldecott who have been victims of sexual abuse, the stay was concluded prematurely. When Siobhan first mentioned her unhappiness and wish to move on, she was not taken too seriously: staff hoped it was a passing phase. It became a proposition worth considering at the tri-annual review. Caldecott was very much against the idea. There was more work to be done and any disruption to Siobhan's schooling was to be avoided. Sheila Calder, the local authority social worker listened more intently but she too hoped that Siobhan would change her mind. Nonetheless, a train of events was set in motion which inevitably would lead to a major transition in Siobhan Kelly's life.

We have previously seen, through Siobhan's eyes, the reasons for her decision to leave. But it is worth rehearsing some of these arguments, particularly as they pose difficult dilemmas for those treating victims of sexual abuse. The initial source of Siobhan's unhappiness was the failure to follow through the abuse disclosure. She was offered further counselling with the specialists at the Community but she declined. The group moved on to other people's problems and Siobhan was left in limbo. As we write, we are not convinced that all of the issues surrounding the abuse have been resolved and some specialist help may be needed in the future.

In other respects, Caldecott was pushing a girl to leave who wanted to stay put. The inevitable expectations that a residential Community has for its children to move on - expectations that are foreign in a natural home - unsettled Siobhan. The idea of independent living, first introduced to her during classes shortly after her fourteenth birthday, was unwelcome. Being clever, not to say manipulative, Siobhan did not want to be independent. Not at 14, not at 18! Suggestions of a move from Woodside to the adolescent unit, Lacton Hall, were also rejected. Her ex-room-mate had moved on to be 'an adolescent' with disastrous consequences. Visiting Mandy in hospital after an overdose or later in a secure unit was enough to convince Siobhan that graduating to a new unit within Caldecott was not suitable. Nor did she want to continue living with a group of younger children with different interests.

These sometimes contradictory influences on Siobhan's thinking unsettled her and she asked to leave. Little happened, even following the review of her progress which was the first formal opportunity to discuss future options. Siobhan then put her foot down. She began to act badly and it was during this period – two and half years after she came to Caldecott – that she stopped keeping a diary for the research team. Still seeing no signs of movement from Caldecott or Sheila Calder, she stopped going to school. Suddenly everybody took notice.

In the previous paragraph, a long and complex process is summarised. For Siobhan it was damaging and adversely affected her schooling. Eventually, people listened and Siobhan got what she wanted. Sheila contacted a local specialist fostering scheme that had placements which would allow Siobhan to remain at the Grammar school. It was at this moment that an element of good fortune entered Siobhan's life which may well be decisive to her long-term well-being. We have emphasised various scientific techniques for predicting outcomes for vulnerable youngsters, but clearly chance and opportunity also play a part.

When Sheila contacted them, the specialist fostering scheme had just completed a recruitment drive. Liz and Steve Felix had applied to be foster parents and seemed to have the qualifications to shelter Siobhan. Liz had ten years experience in work at a psychotherapeutic centre for damaged children. She had moved to Kent to marry Steve, a teacher at a local comprehensive with long experience of children with special educational needs. The couple knew of Caldecott and visited to make Siobhan's acquaintance.

They quickly formed an attachment to Siobhan and she to them. As they knew something about the therapeutic environment and the needs of troubled children they easily negotiated access to Woodside and eased any misgivings that staff might have harboured about Siobhan's impending departure. Steve and Liz soon became regular visitors and, although it was seldom spoken of – and when it was mentioned the possibilities were played down – all hoped that a foster placement could be arranged.

There were, in fact, considerable obstacles to overcome. Sheila Calder and the managers of the specialist fostering scheme had doubts about the ability of Liz and Steve to take on Siobhan as their first foster child. In any case, the couple had to complete the lengthy vetting procedures. Tired of waiting, Siobhan was being a nuisance and threatening to leave school. In haste, a placement was found with experienced foster parents, Ron and Mary Davey, who lived 20 miles away.

The move was extremely difficult for Siobhan. She had an emotional leaving party at Caldecott. On her first night away she felt an enormous sense of loss and acute loneliness caused by living for the first time in several years away from a large group of noisy people. She desperately missed Kate Edwards, Woodside's manager, and to a lesser extent the other key workers and residents. Siobhan had grown used to firm discipline at Woodside and different rules and expectations were unsettling. In trying to impose their own order, the foster parents tried to restrict contact with Caldecott and with the Felix's, who were also keeping up an interest in Siobhan's progress. This strategy eventually undermined the stability of the placement.

Our conversations with Siobhan at that time centred on her desperation to get away from the foster home and her frustration at being denied access to Caldecott and the Felix family. Behind the scenes, a lot of work was being undertaken to secure the Felix family as Siobhan's next foster parents, and urgency was added by threats of overdoses and refusal to go to school. It is difficult to convey the delight that Siobhan expressed on hearing the news that she was going to live with Liz and Steve Felix or the love that she had developed for her new foster parents. If Siobhan could have chosen anywhere in the world to live, it would have been with Liz and Steve and, as she had abandoned any hope of being placed with them, the move was literally a dream come true. As the new parents were sympathetic to the aims and objectives of Caldecott, a certain continuity of experience was achieved and visits to the Community - only three miles away - were once again routine.

Conclusion: Caldecott's contribution to Siobhan's life

At the point of departure, what had Siobhan achieved from her 30 months at Caldecott? She had certainly enjoyed a period of stability and security, safe from the people who had abused her. She had managed fully to disclose the nature of this maltreatment and had formed trusting relationships with people who would listen sympathetically to her story.

Educationally, Siobhan excelled and moved from Caldecott to the local Grammar school which gave her the opportunity to fulfil a considerable potential. Against this, we have also made criticisms of the Community's work, particularly their failure to follow through the disclosure of abuse and their neglect of the family situation. It is noticeable that during discussions surrounding Siobhan's leaving of Caldecott, questions of access and contact with home seldom achieved a salience.

Had Siobhan been placed elsewhere, would she have fared any better? It is difficult to envisage her remaining at home where she was at high risk of further sexual abuse and was refusing to go to school. A less intensive residential centre, such as that which sheltered her brother Nigel, was possible but we know that little progress was made with regard to his understanding of his abuse, and his education was neglected. On the other hand, Nigel's family relationships were better maintained than Siobhan's and reunion with his mother seems highly likely in the long-term. A placement with good foster parents, such as Steve and Liz Felix, combined with counselling from a good psycho-therapist or psychiatrist, might have been possible but the substitute home would have come under immense pressure from Siobhan's misbehaviour and self harm. It is doubtful that she would have built-up enough confidence in a therapist fully to disclose. After all, Siobhan had been seeing Dr Hirshi for several years prior to arriving at the Community. Some local authorities might have tried for adoption but as research shows that the breakdown rate for cases of her age and circumstance is nearly 45%, this would have been a high risk strategy. So we might conclude that Caldecott helped Siobhan as much as, if not more than, any other available option.

Earlier in the study, we set out some conditions necessary for the effective treatment of troubled children. For victims of sexual abuse we stressed the importance of developing the child's sense of security. This has clearly been achieved in the case of Siobhan. We emphasised the need for patience during the process of disclosure, which Caldecott certainly managed well, putting up, as they did, with considerable difficulties during Siobhan's stay. If there was a deficiency in Woodside's care plan, it was in the follow through of the disclosure to treatment.

We also hypothesised that where the treatment plan focuses on the particular needs of the child; where the treatment approach encourages the child to understand the way in which the family contributed to his or her difficulty and involves the family in that process; and where goals set for the child's stay at Caldecott are followed through, outcomes will be optimal. Again, these conditions were largely met in the case of Siobhan and, setting aside the neglect of her family frequently mentioned in this report, we would expect her to do well in the long-term.

The reader can judge Siobhan's situation at the end of the research period and decide whether our hypotheses hold up. We would say that she is doing as well as could be expected given her background circumstances and career route. She is doing far better than some other children from Caldecott on this pathway. The transition into adulthood is going to be difficult. She has to be able to establish satisfying emotional relations; she will probably continue her education, involving a difficult transition away from Liz and Steve. She has to resolve her disputes with mum, Nigel and the other brothers. There are more challenges to come but Siobhan is well placed to tackle them.

Progress of 1986-1990 leavers

Eventually, all children placed at Caldecott must move on. Some, like Trevor Newington, described in the opening section, may remain in touch for many years but there is a formal day of departure and a life to develop afterwards. What happens next? In this section we chart the progress of the 60 children who graduated from the Community between 1986 and 1990. Later, we judge their outcomes against what we might expect for them by virtue of their careers prior to joining the Community. Finally, we try to assess the contribution of Caldecott to these children's lives.

The task is not as straightforward as it first may seem. Even a simple charting of children's progress is complicated by the context in which the departure occurs. Two factors are particularly important, first the child's age, second the reasons for departure. Unlike most follow-up studies in which children leaving a treatment programme are roughly the same age, those moving on from Caldecott can be anything between 10 and 19. The following graph illustrates this wide distribution. Naturally, expectations for an 11 year old graduate are likely to be different from those for an older adolescent. This variation in age reflects the circumstances surrounding children's departure from the Community.

Graph 7: Age of 1986-1990 leavers at the point of departure

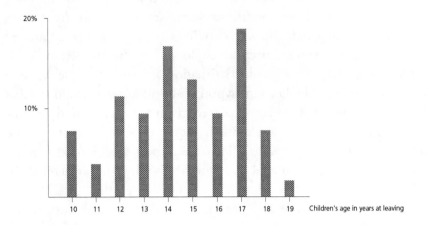

Children's age in years at leaving

We found that in three-fifths of cases at least one of the parties concerned with the child's future expressed misgivings about the decision to leave. The Community itself was the most likely group to have doubts, often feeling that progress was not to greater things but to a more mainstream (and cheaper) placement. In some cases, such as the six per cent in which dissatisfied agencies withdrew the child, the parting was acrimonious. In others, Caldecott staff and local authority workers harboured doubts about the wisdom of acceding to the wishes of some young people to return home, and sometimes young people wished to remain at the Community when the agencies felt they should move on. For every three young people who left at the planned end of their placement, four left early: one left of their own volition; one was excluded, one was withdrawn by his family and one was moved on by one agency against the wishes of another.

Table 9 : Circumstances surrounding the departure of 1986-1990 leavers

Who initiated departure?		Most common reason
All parties agreed	39%	Placement has reached a natural and/ or planned end
Young person	19%	Wish to return to family home
Caldecott	13%	Young person beyond control
Family	13%	Unable to bear separation
Education authority	11%	Progress allows return to mainstream or day special school
Social services	6%	Dissatisfied with progress

Thus young people leave Caldecott at all ages, in a wide variety of circumstances, and frequently against good advice or without good wishes. This knowledge must inform any discussion of children's likely experiences on leaving.

With this background information in mind, we now describe what happened to the 60 children who left Caldecott between 1986 and 1990. The results may be surprising. We have previously commented on the unrealistic perceptions professionals can have for those leaving treatment settings. Most workers are reliant on knowledge about the cases that went badly wrong or those who regularly keep staff in touch about their achievements. As in any study, the more sophisticated the information gathered, the more the results will tend towards equivocation. This does not, however, prevent the analysis from providing some clear messages for practice.

General themes

At the outset, it seems fair to say that *all* 60 children benefited in *some* way from their stay at Caldecott. Part of the follow-up involved gathering information from staff at the Community, many of whom could recall the child, his or her principal problems and Caldecott's contribution to the child's life. This may sound a small achievement but it is more than could be claimed for many other residential centres sheltering children.

Not all the skills acquired at Caldecott are desperately relevant. 'Ah, we taught him to play the piano,' said James King of a boy who ended up in prison. But he was probably one of the few men inside with this skill, his rendering of 'Bird in a Gilded Cage' no doubt brightening many a dull evening. Most of the benefits bestowed by virtue of placement at Caldecott were more obvious, especially for those gaining instrumental skills such as learning to read and write, drive a car or interact easily with adults.

Once leaving Caldecott most leavers go home, although there is some variation by age. Younger graduates are much more likely to return immediately to relatives than those departing in later adolescence. Of those leaving the Community before their fouteenth birthday, 70% went back to the parental home. The other young leavers all went to residential settings, half to children's homes and half to boarding special schools.

For the middle-age leavers, those aged between 14 and 16 years, the pattern was reversed, with the majority (52%) going on to some form of substitute placement, usually foster care for the girls and residential care for the boys. Two out of five (38%) of this group returned home, with the remaining ten per cent finding various forms of supported lodgings. Of those staying at the Community after their sixteenth birthday, nearly all (93%) went on to some form of independent or semi-independent lodgings – generally flats and bedsits in the area around Ashford rather than in their home towns.

If we take another snapshot view two years later, some of the children have moved on. Perhaps justifying the fears of social workers and Caldecott staff, a quarter of the young leavers who returned to parents subsequently experienced breakdown and moved on to children's homes or boarding schools. Of the middle-age leavers aged 14–16 years, those who returned to parents found stability and remained at home throughout the follow-up, but the experience of those who left Caldecott for other substitute care settings was marked by frequent placement change and progressive estrangement from society. All eleven 14–16 year old graduates to residential or foster care had a series of failed placements. Three had the worst outcomes of the 60 leavers – two were in young offender institutions after two years and a third was killed when riding in a stolen car.

More encouraging news can be told about the older leavers who remained at the Community past school-leaving age. We saw that most left to flats and bedsits locally and, two years on, all were managing to keep their heads above water. In the interim, one young person had returned to relatives and some of the others had resurrected family contacts. Generally, dependence on home was closely associated with graduates' ability to achieve a sense of independence. The continued support of Caldecott outreach workers was helpful to the long-term well being of these young people.

This initial scrutiny shows that it is the youngest and oldest leavers who fare relatively well after Caldecott. They do much better than those in the middle-range, that is 14–16 years on leaving, who experience more moves, more placement breakdowns and more general unhappiness. For all of the groups, the importance of a stable placement between the fifteenth and seventeenth birthday is clear. Where this can be provided by the Community, young people are equipped to achieve a level of independence and, more importantly, to survive on their own subsequently. Where permanence and continuity can be provided by parents or foster parents, the situation is also comparatively stable, with the young people gaining in social and survival skills that improve their long-term life chances. Where neither the Community nor parents can hold onto a young person, the prognosis is very worrying indeed. For this group, with a few exceptions, the future consists of a series of increasingly controlling residential placements, including young offender institutions.

Family and social relationships

Similar patterns emerge for leavers' family and social relationships. Most children stayed in touch or resurrected contact with relatives but a proportion remained isolated throughout the follow-up. Generally, leavers who saw relatives regularly had more stable living arrangements. There were again differences in these patterns by age at the point of departure. Those departing before the minimum school-leaving age either lived with their parents or moved around social services and education placements and saw their parents very rarely, if at all. Of the middle-range graduates between 14 to 16 years of age, three-fifths (62%) saw their parents less than monthly and a third had no contact at all. By contrast, those remaining at the Community beyond their sixteenth birthday, though the least likely to live with their parents, were the most likely to have frequent contact with home. The picture for the older leavers was of regular visits and telephone calls, often overcoming considerable barriers and covering greater distances than existed for children of other ages. Four-fifths of those moving to independence display some dependence upon and benefit from good links with parents and other relatives. Although family and social relationships for the older group were rarely unproblematic, links were at least enduring and usually improved.

Support from family members is important for leavers but so is continued help from the Community. We found that it was the older leavers, especially those living away from relatives, who stayed in touch with Caldecott, either with friends made during their stay or with members of staff. Of the younger leavers only two had any such contact. The middle-age leavers moved frequently, so they too tended to lose touch. By comparison, the older graduates, many of whom remained in the Ashford area, frequently visited and received help. Fourteen of the 16 in this group remained in contact with staff and were especially reliant on the outreach workers provided by the Community.

One measure of Caldecott's success is leavers' ability to form positive relationships with people their own age. We know from other child-care research that a young person's peer group influences offending behaviour and the propensity to take advantage of education opportunities or find a job. For the 1986-1990 graduates, the overall picture is generally favourable. Three-quarters made new friends to add to a social network which, as we have seen, often includes family and friends from Caldecott. Those living away from home tended to have the most extensive group of friends. These findings are encouraging, especially when compared to the well-documented isolation of some adolescent care leavers.

Evidence on the quality of relationships is less optimistic. Two-fifths of leavers were involved with groups on the margins of society which led to some petty crime, an anti-authoritarian stance and experimentation with drugs. Once again, the 14-16 year old leavers were the most vulnerable, with the majority drifting towards troublesome groups. It was the older graduates who were most likely to find wide and orthodox social networks and were, therefore, least likely to find themselves in conflict with landlords, employers and the law.

Health, education and employment

We also gathered information on the health of Caldecott's leavers. Naturally, this is an issue of more concern to agencies and parents than to the young people themselves. We had no reason to expect any particular health difficulties and where they did exist, most were self-inflicted. For example, two-fifths (43%) of young men living away from home two years after departing the Community were using illegal drugs, and one or two had serious alcohol problems.

For the young women, by contrast, contact with the health services was usually associated with pregnancy rather than with illness. Nearly two in five (38%) of female graduates had given birth to a child within two years of leaving the Community, and the majority of these children were born to mothers under the age of 16 years, the youngest being 14. All the mothers were living with their babies at follow-up, and apparently coping well. However, their future was hardly what parents, Caldecott staff and other professionals would have hoped for them.

Some of the leavers were old enough to get a job. Our expectations in this area, based on previous research, were not high. Many of the best treatment regimes markedly improve family relations or reduce offending behaviour but few seem to encourage young people to find or hold down a job. The focus of this study is on those whose capacities to find and retain work had often been judged by Caldecott staff (and the research team) as poor, particularly as their education had been disrupted. Our pessimism was ill-founded. Of those old enough to work, all but one found full-time employment for at least part of the two year follow-up and most stayed in work throughout this period. This finding is all the more surprising given the well-known difficulties facing all school-leavers in the early 1990s and the additional disadvantages that Caldecott graduates have to overcome. Several of the girls, for example, combined full or part-time employment with child-care. It was not a case of families finding young people jobs, getting them up in the morning and nagging them to work when more immediate pleasures beckoned. Rather, the evidence speaks for the self-motivation of Caldecott graduates and the efforts of the Community and other agencies in building up their self-esteem and enhancing social skills. Together, these allow young people to interact successfully in a work setting.

We might hope that those not in employment would remain in the education system. Given Caldecott's commitment to schooling, our expectations here were higher. But, while outcomes were better than for most other social services contexts, there was room for improvement. The transition from special to mainstream education was achieved for nearly half of the younger leavers but their prospects were not rosy. For a third, (31%) of the middle-age group, the Community provided the last formal education in the child's life. Once again, prospects for children of this age were worse than for their older counterparts, a quarter of whom went on to some form of further or higher education.

The child's placements subsequent to Caldecott clearly influenced schooling. Those who returned to live with families were not only the most likely to continue their education but they were also the most likely to find a niche in a mainstream school. The 14-16 year old graduates who drifted around foster placements and other residential settings seldom received a satisfactory education, some receiving only a few hours 'home tuition'. For these children, any progress that Caldecott is able to make with school work is quickly unravelled.

Remaining at school, of course, is only half the battle. A more important question is whether the young people benefit from their attendance. We cannot comprehensively answer this question as our data on the 60 children was limited to one important aspect of school success – qualifications. Once again, our findings are encouraging when compared with other settings for vulnerable children and are best for those who were able to continue at the Community up to and beyond their sixteenth birthday. A third of those leaving Caldecott after this point had gained some form of academic qualification. Naturally, those with certificates were more likely – three times more likely – to find suitable and enduring employment during the follow-up period.

Behaviour

In other longitudinal studies we have found that even when leavers from residential care have been able to find work or education opportunities, these are easily wrecked by involvement in crime or general misbehaviour. While not overtly delinquent, a third of the 1986-1990 leavers (40% of boys, and 31% of girls) exhibited bizarre or disturbed behaviour after leaving the Community, the consequences of which were frequently serious, including placement breakdown and loss of jobs. The behavioural problems that had led social workers and educationalists to seek a place at the Community were likely to recur after leaving, though usually with less severity. Older leavers who completed their full term at Caldecott and moved to placements near to the Community and away from home were the least likely to get themselves into trouble.

The leavers we studied were at the peak age for offending behaviour so we expected some to come into contact with the police. Two-fifths (38%) of the boys and one in eight girls were known to have offended during the follow-up period, though fewer (27% of the boys, 6% of the girls) were actually convicted or cautioned. Nearly all of those finding themselves in court had left the Community below the age of 16. Once again, it is the middle-age graduates who do badly and we were disturbed to find that 84% of boys who left Caldecott during their fouteenth or fifteenth year had been convicted within the following two years.

Conclusions

In this section, we have described the general outcomes for the 60 children and young people who left Caldecott between 1986 and 1990. We have seen that the context surrounding the child's departure, especially his or her age and the level of agreement about whether the Community has achieved its aims and objectives, very much influence future progress. Those who move on under a cloud in the few years before they are due to leave school suffer in several ways. They experience return difficulties, are the least likely to take education or employment opportunities and are the most likely to experience placement breakdowns, get in trouble with the police and suffer health problems.

By contrast, younger leavers who return to relatives and older leavers who live away from home and draw on a wide support network of family friends, Caldecott staff and other professionals do relatively well. Let us not overstate these outcomes: the graduates of Caldecott are hardly model citizens and even the older leavers are coping in an adult world of jobs and babies when their more fortunate peers are commuting between University, home and vacations laden with dirty washing, broken hearts and overdrafts for parents. Nonetheless, compared with outcomes from other treatment institutions, the findings are encouraging, particularly with respect to education, employment, social and anti-social behaviour and health.

There are already messages of practical value to be drawn from the findings of the follow-up. A partnership between the Community, parents and others who can support the child after Caldecott is likely to be beneficial. This is true for the majority of children who return home and for those who manage away from relatives and social services placements. 'Independence' for these young people actually means dependence upon family members, upon Caldecott staff and other resources.

The last pages would also suggest that more could be done in preparing young people for adulthood. Caldecott already does more than most, indeed Siobhan felt that they did too much. But a small amount of effort in this area especially with those who intend to live away from relatives, is likely to reap considerable rewards. We do not want to castigate excessively those leaving the Community who become young mothers, get in trouble with the police or use drugs or alcohol. Most are reasonably happy but their overall quality of life could be greatly enhanced if they were better able to plan for their future. Put more simply, their circumstances are not those we would wish for our own children.

Though more comprehensive than other evidence on long-term outcomes on graduates from therapeutic communities, this evidence remains inconclusive. Perhaps the good outcomes reflect the relative tranquillity of some children's situations on entry to Caldecott? Maybe the progress made by younger leavers can be attributed to the support of parents and that of the older graduates to the efforts of local authorities; perhaps Caldecott's contribution is incidental to good outcomes. It is to these gaps in our picture of the Caldecott Community that we next turn.

Career and outcome

Earlier we identified four career routes taken by children arriving at Caldecott. We were able to show from this evidence firstly that children's needs change over time, and secondly, that residents at the Community did not form a homogeneous group. A third function of monitoring career paths is that we can gauge outcomes against the circumstances that propelled the child to Caldecott in the first place. While some delinquency might be expected for children with conduct disorders on entry, it would be a source of concern to find victims of sexual abuse becoming serious criminals. Similarly, not too much can be hoped for the family relationships of children whose upbringing has been extensively disrupted, whereas we know from other research that very young offenders almost always return home.

The four career routes we identified were:
- Children from fragmented families
- Victims of chronic sexual abuse
- Children with behavioural difficulties
- Long-term protection cases.

Children from fragmented families

Children from fragmented families by definition possess by far the fewest family resources of all Caldecott residents. Whilst the young people often experience this as loss, given the quality of the households, *some* distance from home can be seen as an advantage. One predictable outcome for this group is that they were twice as likely as other residents to stay long at Caldecott. Two-fifths (42%) remained at the Community beyond the statutory minimum school leaving age. Expectations were also confirmed by the younger leavers on this career route who were only half as likely to rejoin their families on leaving as other graduates of the same age. Given that nearly all premature leavers want to go home, it is clear that many young people in this category are simply unwanted by their parents, even after the extended respite offered by the Community.

Some early departures by children from fragmented families were understandable. A third of those going before their 16th birthday did so at the request of the education authority which, impressed by improvement in school performances at the Community, placed the child back at home and in a mainstream school. Another fifth of early departures from this group were precipitated by the children themselves who felt secure enough to return home. At follow-up, these young people were generally very settled, suggesting that they had made much progress despite occasional reservations about the child's departure.

Outcomes for the remaining young returners on this career route, all boys, were poor indeed. With no viable home base to turn to, departure from Caldecott was often marked by increasingly strained relations between staff, social services and education. Like Stephen Bozzi, this frequently culminated in the child's exclusion, withdrawal by the local authority or, occasionally, by the refusal of the young person to continue at the Community. Further substitute homes were found, often in crisis, and further movement and school breakdown were common. Children in this category experienced five further placements on average over the next two years, and some had many more.

The best outcome within this group occurs for those who last the distance at the Community and stay into their late teens. They move on to flats and bedsits in the Ashford area where they do well; they are much less likely to offend and more likely to be employed. Parental contact is frequent and the quality of family relations improves, partly because of the young person's absence from home and sense of independence.

Outcomes for children from fragmented families are predictable, except that a proportion of younger leavers unexpectedly find stability back with birth relatives. The findings suggest that children in this group who falter at the Community should not be allowed to drift into other substitute care settings and that exclusion by Caldecott will almost certainly lead to very poor outcomes. Progress for children on this career route is summarised in the following diagram.

Diagram 1: Outcomes for children from fragmented families

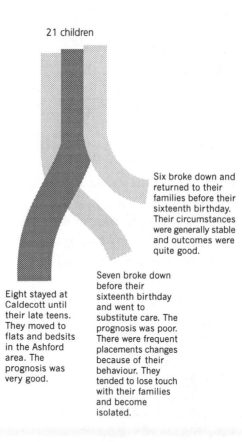

21 children

Six broke down and returned to their families before their sixteenth birthday. Their circumstances were generally stable and outcomes were quite good.

Eight stayed at Caldecott until their late teens. They moved to flats and bedsits in the Ashford area. The prognosis was very good.

Seven broke down before their sixteenth birthday and went to substitute care. The prognosis was poor. There were frequent placements changes because of their behaviour. They tended to lose touch with their families and become isolated.

Victims of chronic sexual abuse

It is harder to generalise about likely outcomes for children who have been sexually abused. Sexual abuse occurs in all types of family and the discovery of maltreatment frequently leads to changes in household membership and relationships. Outcomes also vary considerably according to the gender of the victim and the hopes and expectations of somebody like Siobhan Kelly are different from those of boys in other units who had also been sexually abused.

Victims of chronic sexual abuse are the most likely to leave the Community before their sixteenth birthday; all the boys stayed just a few years at Caldecott. A period for disclosure and some counselling while circumstances at home changed to the extent that the child could return, were generally sufficient. Caldecott fully supported these changes as being in the best interests of the young people concerned. For the girls, however, departure was more likely to be provoked by the child's behaviour, which was often highly sexualised and threatening to the Community. Sometimes, social services, sensing a deteriorating situation, withdrew the child early.

Victims of chronic sexual abuse who leave Caldecott before school leaving age are ill equipped to live independently but they tend to be resilient. Among the four careers identified, they were the least likely to have offended at follow-up (even allowing for gender differences), the most likely to have completed or to have remained in school and the most likely to have gained qualifications, despite their relative youth. In contrast to other leavers, their peers are usually of a sort who would be welcome in most households. So, despite our fears, when we look at the sexually abused leavers two years after departure from Caldecott, most are characterised by stability, hard work and steady progress.

That the girls experienced more disruption than the boys can be largely attributed to their sexual behaviour. Half became mothers during the follow-up, despite being still at school. After two years, all were living with their babies and all were apparently coping reasonably well. However, the birth of a new generation to mothers who are still legally children themselves hardly bodes well for the future. This evidence reminds us of the powerful threat Siobhan's sexuality was to her general good progress. The prospects for the victims of chronic sexual abuse are summarised in the next diagram.

Diagram 2: Outcomes for victims of chronic sexual abuse

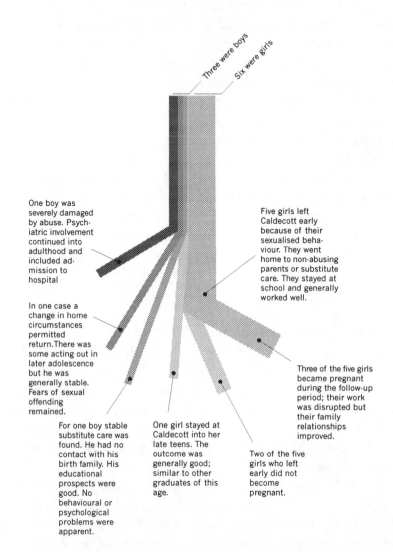

Three were boys

Six were girls

One boy was severely damaged by abuse. Psychiatric involvement continued into adulthood and included admission to hospital

Five girls left Caldecott early because of their sexualised behaviour. They went home to non-abusing parents or substitute care. They stayed at school and generally worked well.

In one case a change in home circumstances permitted return. There was some acting out in later adolescence but he was generally stable. Fears of sexual offending remained.

Three of the five girls became pregnant during the follow-up period; their work was disrupted but their family relationships improved.

For one boy stable substitute care was found. He had no contact with his birth family. His educational prospects were good. No behavioural or psychological problems were apparent.

One girl stayed at Caldecott into her late teens. The outcome was generally good; similar to other graduates of this age.

Two of the five girls who left early did not become pregnant.

Children with behavioural difficulties

As we saw earlier, most children with behavioural difficulties are a little older on arrival at Caldecott than other residents, having caused disruption in other special schools and having been long known to educational psychologists. Their relationships with parents, by contrast, are relatively good. It is clearly difficult for the Community to break the pattern of movement. Two thirds (64%) of this group left before the age of 14, usually due to the pressure put on education authorities by families for a more mainstream placement. The departure frequently occurred against the advice of Community staff.

Ironically, Caldecott's success at containing and reforming these young people was often taken as evidence that they were inappropriately placed. Two-thirds of these early leavers returned home and did reasonably well, thus confirming the perspectives of social workers who doubted the need for an intensive placement like Caldecott. For the others, however, who move to boarding special schools and foster homes, the follow-up study revealed deteriorating family relationships, a high dependence upon residential care and poor educational progress. The Community's unheeded warnings for these children should be read as more than mere self-interest.

Some young people on this career route stayed a little longer and departed in the two years before they were due to leave school. Their outcomes are no better than the early leavers just described who fail to find a niche at home. Far more encouraging are the results for the fifth (21%) of children with behavioural difficulties who stayed at Caldecott until their late teens. These youngsters made a smooth transition from education to employment, maintain meaningful and frequent contacts with home and established stable places to live. These young people had quite clearly benefited from the Caldecott intervention.

These findings are summarised in the following diagram. Readers will note the low levels of delinquency for all children on this career path, a surprising, if welcome, finding. The results once again emphasise the importance of strong family ties and of achieving a smooth transition from the Community to new living situations.

Diagram 3: Outcomes for children with behavioural difficulties

20 children

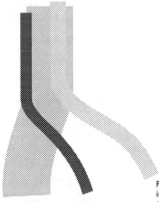

Thirteen were removed by parents or LEAs before their 14th birthday and returned home.

Arrangements for three broke down when they were aged between 14 and 16.

Four remained at Caldecott into their late teens. Their outcomes were among the best. They made a smooth transition from school to work; they had a wide circle of friends and good relations with their parents. There was very little offending.

Four experienced further family breakdown.

At home most did reasonably well. Their relations with their parents improved. They were not delinquent but socially isolated. Their presenting problems were diminished but not eliminated.

In residential care outcomes were poor. There was a tendency for them to be institutionalised. They were unable to manage independently and, despite contact with families, could not live at home either. Their behaviour continued to be disturbed.

Long term protection cases

In contrast to children from fragmented families, professional concerns for the long term protection cases generally focused upon the quality rather than the quantity of family supports. Child protection concerns, usually about physical and emotional maltreatment, were apparent in review papers and relations between families and social services were invariably so poor that a care order had been taken to safeguard the child's future. In addition, the young people themselves had often presented problems of control, more often in school than in the home community. The prognosis for these children was poor on many fronts.

The hostility of the parents and, frequently, the children towards statutory agencies, combined with the behaviour of the residents, frequently led to a premature departure from the Community for this group. Three-quarters left Caldecott before their 16th birthday, although many had been resident for several years at this point.

In contrast to children from fragmented families, long term care cases were more likely to return home. However, whereas the fragmented families had settled down during the child's absence in Caldecott and tended to be supportive thereafter, long-term child protection cases were reunited with volatile relatives who increased the vulnerability of their offspring. For many young people, the good work of the Community was overturned in a matter of weeks. The young people quickly re-established an active role in the family's economic and psychological life, which included violence, burglary and other problems. All early leavers on this career route had been convicted within two years of leaving the Community and the worst outcomes, including custodial sentences and the child who died, occurred after a return to relatives.

The outcomes for those on this career route who move when young from Caldecott to other substitute care settings are little better. A good foster home or a stable residential centre which encourages education and employment and keeps offending behaviour to a minimum can help but continued movement is common. Even those who stayed long at Caldecott tended to experience continued difficulty, although some who cut themselves off from birth families established a modicum of stability.

These findings are summarised in the following diagram. Children who have been long in care before coming to Caldecott represent a small but growing proportion of the Community's work. The evidence suggests that the Community seldom provides stability and protection for these children and that progress made is quickly undone. Employment and education opportunities are rarely taken, delinquency is common and family relationships remain volatile. Re-thinking strategies for these children is advisable. Our expectations for their future were never great but at the end of the study we were left feeling that more could have been done.

Diagram 4: Outcomes for long-term protection cases

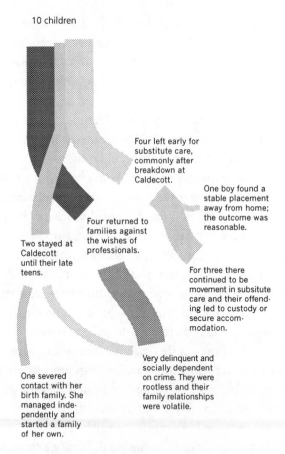

10 children

Four left early for substitute care, commonly after breakdown at Caldecott.

One boy found a stable placement away from home; the outcome was reasonable.

Four returned to families against the wishes of professionals.

Two stayed at Caldecott until their late teens.

For three there continued to be movement in subsitute care and their offending led to custody or secure accommodation.

One severed contact with her birth family. She managed independently and started a family of her own.

Very delinquent and socially dependent on crime. They were rootless and their family relationships were volatile.

A Life Without Problems?

Conclusions

We have now considered outcomes for the 60 children leaving Caldecott between 1986 and 1990 from two perspectives. In the previous section we described progress made and highlighted important contextual factors, such as age and circumstance surrounding departure. In this section we have compared outcomes for children on four career routes, showing that some behaved as predicted while others are doing better or worse than might have been expected. We have not made much of the children's social class and ethnic background as these factors were subsumed by other influences on career. Gender, however, is still a powerful explanatory variable, particular for victims of child sexual abuse.

Clearly, the Community is doing better with some children than with others and we have highlighted weaknesses in their interventions with selected groups. The best progress is made by children from fragmented families and those with behavioural difficulties. The long-term child protection cases, by contrast, seldom adapt to life away from Caldecott and gains made by the Community are frequently lost in the months after leaving. Some of the findings have been surprising. The potential for petty crime and involvement in drugs by children from fragmented families and the possibility of social isolation for the children with behavioural difficulties are two examples of unexpected outcomes.

These findings also tell us much that is generally applicable to work with troubled and troublesome children both within Caldecott and beyond. The major difficulty seems to be getting through mid-adolescence without problems; indeed, the rewards for hanging onto children through this difficult period are considerable. It is not easy to cope with violent children or those who are promiscuous in their early teens and it may be that the Community cannot do the job alone. However it is achieved, avoiding a child's premature departure is vital and rejection should never be allowed to happen.

We have once again seen the value of regular contact with children's families throughout the Caldecott stay. There is practical value in arranging access for almost all of the Caldecott children; it helps to ease the reunion of the early leavers; it helps to maintain a high quality of life for young adults who choose to live away from home; it might help convince parents of children with behavioural difficulties that there are dangers in removing their children early; and it could help avoid the unhelpful reunions of some long-term protection cases. The benefits of regular contact will be felt not only by the children and their relatives but also by Caldecott staff and professionals outside the Community.

Table 10: Summary of outcomes by career pathway

Career route	Likely outcome	Positive areas	Potential weaknesses
Children from fragmented families	Quite good if Community provides stability between 14 and 17 years	Employment; ability to look after self	Drugs; petty crime
Victims of chronic sexual abuse	Generally good, danger of disruption following sexual activity	Education; resilience; gregariousness; orthodox social network	Pregnancy; re-abuse
Children with behavioural difficulties	Mixed. Some problems endure, but most likely to integrate fully	Education; family relationships	Social isolation
Long-term protection cases	Generally poor	None	Offending leading to custody

We have also identified a very small group of children who should not or will not return to relatives in the long-term. These, too, deserve careful strategies to enhance their life chances. Contact with selected relatives might be reduced or even severed and appropriate treatment interventions, including counselling, offered. As important, the Community would need to work in partnership with other agencies that could provide support well into adulthood: Caldecott cannot do this alone. Finally, the last few pages have been a reminder – if one were needed – that progress with children such as those placed at the Caldecott Community is achieved by slow, steady work focused on the particular needs of individual children. We have tried to show how such needs coalesce in four career groups. Expectations should be modestly high. We cannot eradicate such children's difficulties, but we can provide a basis of good self esteem, reasonable family and social relationships and good education and employment prospects. If the Community can do this and offer support in times of crisis, then its graduates probably can do the rest themselves.

Caldecott's contribution to good outcomes

In this, the last of three sections considering outcomes from the Community, we seek to discern the particular value of Caldecott's intervention. Given their circumstances on entry, leavers appear to do relatively well. However, it may be that the children would have developed satisfactorily wherever they had been placed. Is it possible, for instance, that simply by removing the child from home and offering the promise of a fresh start, a previously poor scenario can be made good? Previous experience with difficult children would suggest that such a proposition is unlikely but it is nonetheless important to undertake comparisons and demonstrate the value of Caldecott's work.

We have several methods to aid us in this task. Most simply, we can compare Caldecott's record with that achieved by other types of placement. More robust is the testing of hypotheses described earlier in the book in which we suggested that certain types of intervention and a focus on the particular needs of troubled children lead to better outcomes. We can use the data collected on the 60 leavers from the Community between 1986 and 1990 for this exercise. The qualitative data on children who entered the Community in 1990 and who were followed-up prospectively adds more authority to our arguments.

Caldecott compared with other care settings

Unfortunately, while much has been written about the theory of therapeutic work with damaged children, hardly anybody has put pen to paper about its effectiveness. Beedell's recent survey *Poor Start, Lost Opportunities, Hopeful Outcomes* is useful in its descriptions of staff predictions of what is likely to happen to the children in their care but it does not tell us what actually occurred. Dartington's previous studies have focused on outcomes but the evidence has been about children in different circumstances and following different career paths from the Caldecott leavers, for example persistent delinquents, children looked after by social services and extremely difficult and disturbed adolescents in secure units. Finding satisfactory comparisons is, therefore, difficult and indicates the need for more research in this area.

In previous sections we have stressed the difficulties faced by those children who leave the Community prematurely. The Caldecott placement breaks down in two-fifths (39%) of cases, a statistic which looks at first glance to be unduly high. But difficult youngsters do put considerable pressure on their carers, as studies of other situations have shown. Berridge and Cleaver found that nearly half (46%) of six to eleven year olds placed in long-term foster homes left early. The following graph, taken from the research of Thoburn and colleagues, shows the proportion of children with special needs being placed in long-term foster or adoption homes breaking down by the age of the child on the day the placement commenced. Against this evidence, we can say that Caldecott is at least as likely to provide stability as other available options.

Graph 8: The proportion of special needs children in long-term foster or adoptive homes experiencing breakdown by the age of the child on commencement of placement

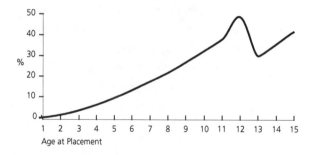

The Community also appears to be more effective than other care settings in equiping its residents for adult life. If we focus momentarily on those children who were 16 years or more on departure from Caldecott, and who attempt to establish themselves away from relatives, we can compare outcomes with the many studies of young people leaving care for independent living situations. This analysis would suggest that Caldecott's young adults are up to four times more likely to find employment, three times less likely to get themselves convicted or into custody and have a slightly better chance of establishing their own house or flat. Levels of pregnancy, although lower, are closer to those found in

A Life Without Problems?

other follow-up studies of vulnerable young people. These data must be treated with considerable caution as we cannot be sure that we are comparing like with like but they do offer some room for optimism.

Better indications of Caldecott's contribution can be gauged by assessing outcomes against the quality of intervention for each of the children followed-up. First however, we need an absolute indicator of outcome. How do we decide that the individual has done well or badly? We have provided a variety of evidence about outcomes for the Caldecott children but can this be summarised in a single indicator?

The answer to these questions has to be 'yes', otherwise we would be left with levels of equivocation that would be unhelpful to those providing and purchasing services at Caldecott. We have brought together the various outcome measures, compared the child's progress with expectations prior to and at the end of the Caldecott sojourn and taken into account the best possible scenario for children on a particular career route. There is however, one further set of information that needs to be included and that is the perspectives of the Caldecott staff, local authority professionals, the children and their families.

As the following table indicates, two years after the child has moved on, levels of satisfaction with Caldecott's contribution remains generally high. In one-fifth (22%) of cases all parties to the placement were pleased about the child's situation and Caldecott's role in achieving this outcome. In only one case was everybody dissatisfied.

Table 11: Satisfaction with Caldecott's contribution to children's well-being two years after departure from the Community

	%
All satisfied	22
Professionals pleased; family or young person equivocal	22
All equivocal	15
Mixed	25
All dissatisfied except Caldecott	15
All dissatisfied	2

We can add to these results comparisons between expected outcomes for the children at the point of entry and actual outcomes two years after leaving. In just under a quarter (23%) of cases, we were satisfied that the child had done as well as could have been expected, given his or her background characteristics and other circumstances. For nearly half (47%) of the children, the outcomes were moderate, suggesting that for the remaining 30% the children did badly. As the following table illustrates, when we compare the overall outcomes of children on the four career pathways, it is those from fragmented families or exhibiting behavioural difficulties who are most likely to do well.

Table 12: Overall outcomes for children by career route

	Good	Moderate	Poor
	N=	N=	N=
Fragmented families	5	11	5
Victims of chronic sexual abuse	2	4	3
Children with behavioural difficulties	6	11	3
Long-term child protection cases	1	2	7
Total	**14**	**28**	**18**

Taking a different perspective and focusing on individual situations, it is possible to compare outcomes with the quality of intervention. To do this, we used the hypotheses on treating troubled children described in previous sections. We suggested that outcomes for the child will be optimal if interventions:

- encourage the child to understand the way in which the family contributed to his or her difficulty
- involve the family in this process
- follow through goals set for the child at successive stages during the stay.

As the following table shows, the Community was successful at meeting two of these criteria in about a half of the cases we studied but only a third of the families were involved in the treatment process in any meaningful way. Getting the intervention right would seem to be important for, where the factors apply, outcomes for individual children are more likely to be good, or at least moderate.

Table 13: Dimensions of the treatment intervention and overall outcome for children at two years

Dimensions of treatment intervention	Factor applies	Proportion where factor applies and outcome at least moderately good
	%	%
Child understands the family contribution to difficulty	53	68
Family involved in the treatment process	31	69
Goals set are followed through	48	61

A better test of our hypothesis is to examine the above criteria in combination. In only some cases were all three dimensions of the hypothesis satisfied. The next table shows that where the child is encouraged to understand the way in which the families contributed to his or her difficulty, where the families are involved in the treatment process and where goals set are acted upon and followed through, outcomes are always at least moderately good and are often optimal. If only some of the conditions apply, outcomes are mixed and if none at all prevail, the prognosis for the child is usually poor.

Table 14: Overall outcomes for children by the number of conditions completed in the recommended treatment plan

Condition	Good	Mixed	Poor
None	N=0	N=4	N=5
Some	1	17	11
All	13	7	2
Total	**14**	**28**	**18**

Outcomes for the children in the intensive study

Earlier in the study we described the situation of the eight children who lived in Woodside with Siobhan. We have been able to watch their progress much more closely than has been possible with the 60 leavers between 1986 and 1990. We have incorporated much of their experience into our thinking and this should be reflected in the findings described in this and the preceding two sections. We will bring the discussion to a close by describing what happened to these children. As we shall see, their experiences shed additional light on some of the ideas explored in this study.

Billy and Brian Adams

Billy and Brian had been admitted to the Community after displaying behavioural difficulties that led to several school breakdowns. Their mother Beatie was not the sort to be pushed off the scene and in any case the boys went home to stay every weekend. The early days were difficult for the children, especially for Brian who was very fragile whenever separated from his older brother. It was extremely difficult, for example, for the researchers to engage these children without upsetting them and much of our data was therefore collected at a distance.

The intervention at Caldecott was focused and, thanks to good liaison with social services, links with home were maintained throughout the boys' stay. Problems occurred when it was suggested that Billy might be a suitable candidate for the adolescent unit at Lacton Hall. Unable to control his anxiety, Billy began behaving badly and Brian soon followed suit. Their request to return home was surprisingly agreed to by mum and, now aged 18 and 16, they are happily settled with her in London. Their ability to form lasting relationships other than with their mother remains a weak spot in their development but in other respects outcomes for these boys were moderately good.

Tina Richmond

Tina had been sexually abused by several members of her family prior to her admission and family links were therefore highly restricted. A breach of trust by her mother during one visit to Tina led to access being severed altogether: mum had taken her to the toilet and attempted to sexually assault her. Not as bright as most, Tina took much longer fully to disclose the nature of her abuse and four years after admission is still undergoing intensive treatment from the team of specialists at the Community, particularly the psychiatrist and psychotherapist.

Understandably, little has been done to involve the family in the treatment process but Tina's progress is as good as can be expected, given her circumstances. Early departure would be disastrous but the Community is finding it difficult to cope with her increasing sexual awareness. If pregnancy can be avoided, the long-term prospects are reasonable.

Tony and Thomas Bozzi

We have already rehearsed the poor outcomes for Thomas Bozzi, who left the Community prematurely after threatening to hit a member of staff with a golf club. Unfortunately, relationships between the Community and Mrs. Bozzi and with the boys' social workers deteriorated to a point that Tony was withdrawn by the local authority a few weeks after his brother. Typically for children from fragmented families who leave Caldecott early, outcomes thereafter were poor with the boys experiencing several placement breakdowns and failed attempts to rehabilitate them with their mother. The Community's contribution in the long-term was negligible although the strategies these boys learnt about legitimate expressions of anger may stand them in good stead.

Keith Taylor

Long in local authority care, Keith came to Caldecott shattered by the premature death of his step-father and the extensive disruption of several attempts of rehabilitation with his mother and five siblings and step siblings. The Community has provided stability for Keith, educational achievement - quite unexpected on entry - and it has also worked very successfully to maintain his links with home. Keith's brothers and sisters were all of an age and disposition that they were welcomed at the Community and, surrounded by her brood, neither was mother intimidated. As a result, relationships between Caldecott, the local authority and the child's home were much better than for other children in the intensive study. Although he is still resident at Caldecott, Keith is working and eventually intends to return to live close to his family home. The prospects for him look reasonably good.

Kevin Clarke

Kevin Clarke came to the Community with his brother Neil. The two never got on with each other, a pattern largely reflecting other poor relationships at home. While Kevin was placed in Woodside, Neil lived in Lacton House, a specialist unit two miles away from the main campus. The behaviour of both boys improved during their early months at Caldecott and staff were concerned with questions of *when* the boys would go home rather than *if*.

Like local authority social workers previously, however, Caldecott was constantly rebuffed in its attempts at rehabilitation. Mrs. Clarke has lived with three different men during her sons' residence at the Community and each partner has turned out to be violent. During one visit to see Kevin, staff were so concerned that they took her to Ashford hospital for a check-up. Apart from an abortive plan to have the boys adopted, Caldecott strategy has progressed reasonably well and, if family links can be maintained, the long-term prognosis should be reasonably good.

Mandy Atkinson

Like Siobhan, with whom she shared a room, Mandy had been sexually abused. Mandy's successful disclosure was followed by a move to the Community's adolescent unit two miles away. After the security and tight boundaries of Woodside, Mandy found it extremely difficult within the more liberal atmosphere at Lacton Hall. Her behaviour deteriorated, she became promiscuous, refused to go to school and experimented with drugs. Before long she had to be admitted to hospital for an overdose of paracetamol, something which might leave her with long-term health difficulties. Mandy's experience was an important influence on Siobhan's decision to leave Caldecott.

Woodside made considerable progress with Mandy, yet much of her development was apparently rapidly undone by moving within the Community. Since leaving Caldecott altogether, she has been placed in a secure unit and her long-term outlook is grim. In many respects extremely similar to Siobhan in characteristics and background, Mandy shows how thin is the dividing line between good and bad outcomes for troubled children.

Hayley Clifton

Hayley left the Community after a stay of nearly nine years; she was 19 years old. During that period, Hayley's parents had drifted out of her life and much of Woodside's efforts in the years before her departure were devoted to preparing her for independence. A local flat was arranged but at the last moment Hayley decided to return to her mother 20 miles away. It was not long before the family had resumed an almost forgotten pattern of rows and disputes but Hayley always seemed happy on her regular visits to Woodside.

Three months after moving on, Hayley told the staff and children that she was pregnant. She was delighted. The father remains unknown but Hayley quickly settled into her new flat close to home, furnished with help from the Community and the Leila Rendel fund and supported by regular visits from Woodside staff. Last we heard, she and her baby, Stan, were doing very well and there were rumours of a second baby on the way.

Conclusions

This evidence concludes our look at outcomes for children placed at Caldecott. The results are generally favourable and, while we have been critical of the Community for the quality of its work with children's families, the cases show how difficult it can be to make gains in this area. The findings are the first of this type for therapeutic communities and hopefully show the value of research in practice with difficult children. We have highlighted the most vulnerable groups, key moments of decision making and ways of maximising the benefit of the Community's treatment regime. These findings should have currency well beyond the walls of Caldecott and will hopefully act as a spur to others to add, challenge or refine the observations made in this part of the study.

Siobhan today

As we write this study, Siobhan has been with Liz and Steve for 12 months. She has just passed eight GCSEs and is about to begin her A levels. The placement is stable and none of the risks associated with children who have been sexually abused have materialised. We cannot be certain that she will progress into adulthood without any problems, but the prognosis is as good as we could hope given her background. She must be counted as a success story although on the day we met her, shortly after arrival at Caldecott, a range of outcomes was possible.

We conclude her story with an essay written about six months into the foster placement. It tells of her life with the foster parents Steve and Liz and describes her family relations. We make a few additional comments on this short piece of work.

Life in a foster home - by Siobhan Kelly, aged 15

Liz and Steve picked me up from Mary's on 5th of September 1993 as planned. I was sad to leave Mary's but the excitement of moving to my new home kept me happy. The first few weeks were successful, what's known as the 'honeymoon period'. School started in September and everything was going well. However it wouldn't be right if I didn't have any problems here, how could I live a life without problems?!

After a few weeks I began to 'test' my new foster parents out. I won't go into how I went about this, but I am sure you can imagine. Liz and Steve remained firm with me. I knew where I stood. I felt safe and that was it. Having discovered I couldn't do as I pleased and Liz and Steve are in charge, I settled again and hiccups are few and far between. Liz and Steve are fair with me and most things are negotiable and I respect them for that.

The pace of life is slower for me. There are still things I miss about Woodside and people I miss, but I wouldn't say that I would like to live back there. I've got used to living in a family environment and living back in an institution would be too demanding for me. One of the advantages of living here is I can have friends over without the worry of children playing up and being restrained, although I give Liz and Steve a lecture on what they can and can't do or say!

Because of their long hours I am alone quite a lot. This was difficult at first but I quite appreciate the space now. I don't see Liz very often but I was warned about that before I came. I have my own room which I've longed for and I like the privacy and space which I didn't get before, when I was in Woodside.

Liz and Steve are always there to talk to if I have any problems, and I don't have to fight for their attention, so gone are the days when I ran away and hurt myself, those kind of thoughts never cross my mind these days.

Since I've been here I've done well in school. Being settled means I can concentrate on my school work. Steve and Liz have high expectations of me which encourages me to do well. Steve, being a teacher, helps with homework, revision, etc. I managed to do well in my mocks, which has made me less worried about the exams in the summer.

My family

I had some visits with them shortly before Xmas. I saw my mum and this went okay apart from Kurt (my eldest brother) turning up, which I found difficult. I saw Adrian and Nigel which was good. I also saw Barry

(2nd eldest). He lives in a flat on his own. He was very depressed with money problems etc. I felt really sorry for him and it really made me appreciate what I've got here. Anyway, shortly after this visit my mum phoned up to tell me Kurt was in hospital after cutting his wrists. Apparently, he was upset after seeing me, and felt guilty about what he'd done when he was drunk. My mum phoned me regularly after this to tell me how badly Kurt was getting on.

I also got a visit from my dad which was deviously planned by Nigel. This shook me up a bit, because now my dad knows where I live I will never feel safe on my own in the house. I phoned Nigel the next day and he didn't even feel guilty about what he'd done. So now it stands that Nigel and I are not talking to each other; well, he knows my number if he wants to phone.

Sometimes I wonder if I didn't have any contact with them at all, I would be much better off. Despite all this I had an excellent Xmas with Liz and Steve and I didn't let things get me down. Things have calmed down a lot now. I think that's about all apart from I am very happy and settled and grateful to Liz and Steve for having me.

Siobhan Kelly

Comment

'How could I live a life without problems?' asks Siobhan. How many of us can claim a life without problems? Siobhan has overcome more than most and possibly has some way to go before she feels completely at ease. The essay captures her situation at the end of the study. A confident, bright person, somebody who is very resilient, she has caused Liz and Steve problems but no more than any adolescent poses for her parents. The essay also revealed a few outstanding features of life at Caldecott that we had missed during our research.

The fact that an institution is very demanding for children is something we overlooked during the study. The general hubbub, the constant comings and goings, the crises to overcome, the group meetings – all this becomes overwhelming. Staff frequently reflect on the relief felt as the echo of the last voice reverberates before the Community goes to sleep. Siobhan hears this echo today, probably with a touch of nostalgia, but certainly with enormous relief. She is glad to have moved on.

The importance of privacy has been charted elsewhere. For all the warmth of Caldecott and the support it provided, Siobhan never had a 'place' to bring her friends to. The current craze among adolescents, inevitably an import from North America, is to 'sleep over'. The prudish need not be alarmed for these events merely involve a rather routine round of young men and women sitting through the night talking, drinking, eating and watching videos, ideally in the absence of any adults who normally live in the house. A sleep over in a residential institution is something a member of staff does to watch over the children. These contrasts are plain to Siobhan.

The family is still a part of Siobhan's thinking, they have not gone away. As Siobhan gets older, she is beginning to worry about them although the sense of danger she feels about her father endures. In time, the family problems may be resolved but it is clear that they will not subside. It is noticeable that the intermittent pattern of access and other contacts established at Caldecott has continued during the foster placement.

Siobhan's comments conclude our look at the Caldecott Community. We have traced its history, considered the characteristics of the children and charted their progress. In this section we have looked at outcomes from several different angles. We now bring the book to a close with some general conclusions, Siobhan's perspective on the research process and some recommendations for the future.

Part Six

Conclusions

"

Siobhan's view

When the early draft of the book was complete, the first people to read it were Siobhan and her foster parents, Steve and Liz Felix. All three visited the Research Unit for the best part of a week. The process of gathering their views – and those of Siobhan in particular – was one which all of us approached with some trepidation. It was the first time Siobhan had read her contribution in the context of the wider report and her first opportuntity to comment on our interpretations of her life and the work of the Caldecott Community. The report was also likely to give Steve and Liz new insights into Siobhan's life. Many of our anxieties were well-founded.

Before we describe the process and the outcomes of our discussions, it is worth briefly recounting the principles we used when collecting information from Siobhan. The work with Siobhan and the data collected was different from that with the other children participating in the study. At the outset, we made an undertaking that, in building up a picture of her life, we would listen only to Siobhan. We did not read Siobhan's file and, while researchers talked extensively to her relatives, social workers and key workers at the Community, this data was not shared with the researcher who worked closely with Siobhan until the point at which we began writing the book. Thus, Siobhan's story is her own story. In this study we see her as she would have us see her. Naturally, we expected there to be gaps and possibly even inconsistencies in this perspective, and the meeting at Dartington to read the report was an opportunity to reflect on these.

Siobhan and her foster parents read the report during the first full day of the visit. Their immediate reaction was almost elation. They liked the report and felt it captured Siobhan and the Community. This was welcome news to the researchers; quite apart from the favourable responses to the research messages, we were conscious that Siobhan always had the right to refuse permission for us to use her contribution, something which would have required us to re-write much of the study.

The second day, however, was much more difficult. Steve and Liz had prepared Siobhan very well for the visit to Dartington and encouraged her to read her old diaries and remember some of the past experiences in Woodside. Nonetheless, the pain for Siobhan of seeing her life described in a book was considerable. The second day they read the book again and discussed the source of her unhappiness. The conclusion they reached was also troubling for them and it is of importance to the evidence described in this report.

Siobhan's diaries describe, as we have commented, the frustration of being unable to disclose abuse and the misbehaviour which is associated with being unable to report maltreatment or simply having nobody to listen. Siobhan's prospects slowly improved during her time at Caldecott but for every two steps forward there was one backwards. Tottering on the precipice of the third floor balcony, hanging by her fingertips from a motorway bridge and taking overdoses of pills could all be explained by her maltreatment and the inability of Siobhan to explain the nature of and understand the consequences of that abuse. Every diary entry therefore means far more to Siobhan than it does to others.

As Steve and Liz talked to Siobhan about this, they realised that they did not know the full extent of her maltreatment and secondly that the story presented in this report is incomplete. There were disclosures, not a disclosure. Siobhan's problems stemmed not only from her sexual abuse but also from emotional neglect, the failure of her mother and other relatives to support, comfort and encourage as well as the absence of somebody in whom she could trust. All of this crystallised as they read the report.

We learn from this that victims of sexual abuse filter information about their lives to the world outside. Only Siobhan knows everything that happened to her. Liz, her foster mother, knows more than anybody else, probably more than Steve, her husband. Caldecott staff who looked after Siobhan are quite well informed and probably know as much as is reported in this book. The field social worker knows less still. There are graduations of knowledge about Siobhan's situation and, while we have got as full a picture as researchers are ever likely to get, it is only part of the story.

On the next day, the researcher who worked with Siobhan throughout the study joined the discussions. This, in itself, was extremely difficult. Prior to this point, the relations between Steve and Liz and Siobhan, and between Siobhan and the researcher had been compartmentalised.

We only knew what Siobhan wanted to tell us. Suddenly, we were thrust into a situation in which parties with very different levels of understanding of Siobhan's situation were talking to each other. Steve and Liz put some pressure on Siobhan to provide the information which would give a fuller explanation of her behaviour at Caldecott; Siobhan and the researcher resisted. The research team does not fully know what happened to Siobhan but we do not feel that the extra details would in any way enhance the messages contained in this report.

We cannot capture the different emotions of Siobhan, her foster parents and the researcher. It was an extremely difficult process which taught us a great deal more about Caldecott and the lives of children it shelters. It also reminds us that taking the child's view seriously is time consuming and needs very careful preparation, understanding and interpretation. That we were able to do it at all at Caldecott says much about the resilience, insight and co-operation of Siobhan and the support of her foster parents. Thus, the process of getting Siobhan to read and comment on the research report went from initial elation, to considerable upset before reaching some *modus vivendi*.

We ended by talking alone to Siobhan about her observations and feelings about the report. We did not record this discussion but the following is a reasonably accurate summary of what she had to say.

> I hated reading the diary. Nobody likes to read what they write about themselves. The worst bit was Steve reading bits out because it didn't seem right. It's horrible to hear it like that.
>
> But I think it's a fair picture of what I am like and what Caldecott is like. I know I didn't tell you everything but nobody tells everything do they? What do I know about you? The bits that are missing are to do with the abuse and not just the sex. Everybody gets hung up on that but it's not always the most important thing.
>
> For all the times I have talked to you, how many times have we talked about sex? Hardly ever. It's not important. But if you go to a therapist that's all they want to know about, and they never talk straight. They say things like, now Siobhan, I remember when I first wore high heels, do you remember the first time anything happened to you? And I think, 'Oh my god, what is this?' So I tell them about the first time I saw *Eastenders*, and when they ask 'any other firsts?', I tell them about *Neighbours*.

I learnt early on not to tell everything. My mum went with us to family therapy once and I said that my dad had given us a belting once. When we got outside my mum gave me such a thrashing for telling the therapist about that. But it's important. There's a girl in school who disclosed and told people in school and every time she does something now people say 'Oh, poor old Tracey, she was sexually abused'. I don't want people thinking that about me. There's more to me than having been abused.

But I know so much more than people in school. They are so naive. Everybody's anti-abortion at the moment and in RE we have a discussion and people say 'well, what if you were raped, would you have an abortion then?' And I think 'Oh my god'. And they say 'what if it was incest?' and some of them say they wouldn't have an abortion then. It's rubbish, they've no idea what they are talking about, but I don't tell them what I know.

Trouble is, as I get older they are less concerned about me. When I first went to Highworth, they thought I was at Caldecott because I had murdered somebody. I told them it was because my mum and dad had split up which isn't exactly untrue, it's just not all the truth. But since I've moved to live with Steve and Liz and I'm in a nice house in a nice village they are not so sympathetic to me. They say 'you're all right now Siobhan' and in some ways I am, but in others I'm not.

You were right to say in the report that there was more to do on the disclosures. There's still more to tell, even Liz doesn't know everything and she knows more than anybody else. But what were they supposed to do? I didn't want to go to any therapist and they can't make you these days. They wanted me to go down to Lacton Hall but there was no way after what happened to Mandy. So I just put my foot down. The child's view is important, you always say that but what I say isn't always what's best for me. You were right as well about my mum. I wanted to see her all the time but it was me saying I wouldn't go or I wouldn't phone. After the overdose, Caldecott staff practically had to hold me down to get me to phone my mum.

The things you miss in this book are all the normal bits that happen to people of my age. Like, I haven't heard from my friends for ages, and I don't know whether anybody likes me at the moment. That's my main worry. And my exam results tomorrow. I'm crapping myself about them. And then there's this really nice bloke at Jubilee Lodge (where Siobhan does voluntary work) but he looks 18 and turns out to be 21 with a girl-friend. And I worry that I'm getting too posh and that I should give up smoking. These are the things that are important to me now and I don't know if that is in the study.

And I still worry a lot about mum and Nigel and my other brothers. Liz and Steve have been really good. They make sure I see mum regularly and they say to you that access is going really well, but it's hard really. We still aren't really talking to each other although we say a lot. I hope that will change, you're right to write that it's something I've still got to do.

But I've done pretty well really. When I look at the other children at Caldecott that you met, I've done better than most of them. And I've done loads better than Mandy although she was a bit like me (although not as alike as you make us seem in the book!) And I've done much better than Nigel who is now in his bedsit with no phone and no job. A lot depends on the exam results tomorrow. If I can get that right I will be OK.

Conclusion

The day after this conversation took place, Siobhan telephoned the re-searchers to say that she had passed all eight of her GCSEs. She has now returned to school to do her A levels and sees a University place as a distant but achievable prospect.

Caldecott in a wider context

Few of us will avoid spending some part of our lives in a residential set-ting. Many of us, after all, enter and depart this life via an institutional bed, and many of the rites of passage of the intervening years are cel-ebrated, or endured, in residence. For some, puberty has its boarding schools, its camps, its adventure holidays and its halls of residence, and marriage too is often consummated in boarding establishments, frequently nowadays in foreign countries. Major life crises - illness, breakdown, divorce, criminal convictions - find us packing our bags and leaving home for hospitals, health farms, hotels, or prisons. Some professionals such as those in the armed forces are periodically in residence for much of their career. Adult reliance on residential settings seems if anything to be in-creasing, but what of children?

There is a wide range of circumstances in which residence may be offered to children. The largest numbers overall – more than a million admissions every year – are young people accommodated by the health service in ordinary hospitals. The most numerous group in residence at any one time are boarders in independent schools; for them the experience may be seen as status-maintaining, career enhancing or as simply enjoyable. Some pupils however have a *need* to board so that their parents can work abroad, cope with nomadic lifestyles or be liberated from deleterious home circumstances. The next largest group, which includes the children in Caldecott, have a similar requirement for an alternative home but coupled with specific welfare and educational needs. For others, such as those sheltered in the penal sector, the need is not so much that of the child or family but that of the wider community which requires protection from delinquent or dangerous adolescents.

An analysis of the needs and numbers of those sheltered in different types of setting can tell much about the likely future of residential care and education. The preceding pages have explored the effectiveness of Caldecott and other therapeutic settings with different groups of children. But if the Community is to prosper, it must establish a niche in the wider context of residential child-care and education and must accommodate pressures for change brought about by social, economic, legal and policy factors. It is no longer enough to believe in residence in its own right; today strategic planning and proof of its viability are needed.

It is well documented that the number of children sleeping in residential establishments in England and Wales is diminishing. In 1971 Moss estimated that there were 236,000 children in residence at any one time. Nearly three-fifths (140,000) were boarders in ordinary schools and a further 15,600 patients in non-psychiatric hospitals. The remaining 80,000 lived in community homes, boarding special schools, residential provision for children with disabilities and prisons. When Parker looked at this last group in 1984 he found a shrinkage in the total residential population, but that falls were unevenly spread across the various sectors. Since then there has been a further decline, so much so that at the beginning of the 1990s, there were only 150,000 children in residential establishments at any one time in England and Wales. In 1971, for every 1,000 children under 18, 20 would have been living away from home and family; by 1991 this figure had fallen to 15.

The reasons for this change stem from a mixture of demographic and policy factors as well as from changes in the preferences of customers. The reduction is most evident in young offender establishments and in services for young people with physical and mental disabilities where alternatives to residence have been introduced, especially by the voluntary sector. The declining popularity of residence is also apparent in independent schools where a growth in the numbers of day pupils, fewer boarders and flexibility in residential styles are increasingly manifest.

In prisons reductions have been largely due to a decline in referrals, whereas in education, child-care and health, turnover has been simultaneously augmented by reductions in the amount of time children spend in institutions; days and weeks have replaced months and years. Hospitals, for example, admit three times as many children annually as they did in 1971, yet the number resident on any one night has declined by 17% over the same period.

Is it possible to generalise about the kinds of children who today might find themselves growing up in an institution? The baby in intensive care, the seven year old unpacking his trunk at a prep school and the teenage delinquent behind bars appear to have little in common beyond separation from parents and home. The attitudes of parents, children and professionals are likewise varied: some greet the offer of a place at a residential institution with champagne and rejoicing, others with tranquillisers and tears. The picture is, then, one of an eclectic system serving a diverse clientele, unified only by the provision of a bed.

On closer inspection, however, some common factors emerge. Firstly, for all their diversity, children in institutions share childhood experiences which depart significantly from the norm. Whether rich, deprived, talented or delinquent, the young people are not typical. Secondly, all will have been placed residentially because their homes and local services cannot meet their perceived needs. In the case of boarders at private schools this judgement has been made by the parents. In other cases, the decision has been made by professionals seeking to protect children from danger, to prevent them harming others or to obtain specialist health or education services.

Questions of resources inevitably mediate between demand and actual provision. There is, for example, considerable geographical variation in the provision of residential facilities and in facilities which might reduce the need for residential placements. The availability of beds introduces another factor, namely timing; the concerns of purchasers introduces another, that of cost. Residential provision is expensive and comparatively inflexible. Where beds are provided, there is pressure to fill them. It would be naive to assume that all children who need an institutional place get one or that all children who occupy an institutional bed actually need or even want it. As a general rule, however, children find themselves in specialised establishments like Caldecott because exceptional circumstances give rise to problems which cannot be met in any other way.

Such demands can stem from the child, his or her family, welfare agencies or the wider society. A conspicuous feature of recent child-care legislation has been a requirement to monitor and inspect what are essentially private arrangements between parties, for example, parents and independent schools. This change is symptomatic of the growing emphasis on the rights of children in local authority accommodation and boarding special schools. A second feature common to all children in residence, then, is their statutory need for protection and respect for their wishes above and beyond that afforded to children living at home with their families. Residential workers, in consequence, are no longer in *loco parentis*, and their relationships to their charges contrast with those of ordinary parents, both legally and emotionally.

There has been a tendency for both supporters and detractors of residence to stress the similarities and to underplay the differences between establishments as diverse as boarding schools, prisons and psychiatric hospitals. For those hostile to residential care, these would include isolation, loss of privacy, regimentation and the formation of powerful inmate cultures. In contrast, outcomes such as independence, sociability, self-control, responsible citizenship and effective leadership are cited by proponents as the very purpose of residential life. Whether residence for children is viewed as enhancing or damaging, few would deny that the residential experience itself can be a memorable and formative experience, whatever the educational, treatment or punishment arguments which justify it.

Residential provision is more frequently used to meet the needs of some groups of children than of others. In 1971, Moss identified six attributes which commonly determined placements and these remain important today. He noted, for example, that residential institutions housed a disproportionate numbers of males. To an extent, this pattern has endured, particularly in special education and youth justice. Caldecott stood against this tide, without much success, by putting a premium on ensuring a genuinely mixed community.

Similarly, in the 1970s, Moss noted that the average age of children in residential provision was rising and the Utting Report has confirmed that long-term residents in child-care and educational establishments are now predominantly adolescents. Residential provision for children of primary school age is now almost entirely on a short term basis and such stays are largely in hospitals. Again, Caldecott is providing something different in its concern for the welfare of younger children. When Moss undertook his work, many children in institutions had disabilities of various kinds. This, too, has changed. A major development since the 1970s is the marked decline in the numbers of children in long stay residential care because of learning difficulties. Many children with behavioural problems, however, are still placed residentially within social services and education provision.

As quiescent children, albeit with special needs, have increasingly stayed at home, so those in residential settings display more acute problems and challenging behaviours. Problems of control, absconding, violence, self-mutilation, sexual abuse, suicide and offending increasingly affect child-care institutions, boarding special schools, psychiatric facilities and youth prisons. The control of difficult behaviour has become the *raison d'être* of much residential work and, again, Caldecott has many ideas and much practice wisdom to offer.

It is also apparent that residence is less homogenous in terms of the religious, cultural and racial affiliations of its residents. It is difficult to arrive at a reliable estimate of the numbers of children from ethnic minorities, or from a mixed ethnic background, currently resident in children's homes and boarding schools but the difficulties of precise analysis cannot hide the fact that children in residential provision reflect a nation no longer monocultural. In these aspects, Caldecott is committed to remain at the forefront of good practice.

One constant, however, is that residential provision still houses disproportionate numbers of children from extremes of the class system. Independent school boarders are still predominantly children from affluent backgrounds and children in state-financed facilities are still predominantly under-privileged. But, even here, things are changing. The association of residence with either great wealth or deprivation is decreasing. One in four boarders at ordinary schools receives help with fees on the basis of need, whilst many children in boarding special schools return to relatively comfortable and loving homes in school holidays.

Summary

Children in residential establishments are not typical of children generally. The numbers of children accommodated have declined steadily and views on the functions of residential provision within wider systems of education, welfare and social control have changed considerably since the Second World War. Anti-institutional sentiments have been influential in all sectors, from orphanages to public schools. Health, education, social services and youth justice policies of community care for less problematic clients have produced a situation where residential establishments increasingly shelter a group of adolescents with considerable emotional, behavioural, learning and other difficulties. These are not so much children for whom residence is seen as the best option among many, but children for whom there are few alternatives. Even in hospitals, for example, beds are only occupied by the acutely ill.

This justification for placing children residentially relies less on questions of moral responsibility and desirability and more on assessments of need. Children are no longer said to be so placed because they deserve it or because they would benefit from residence but increasingly because they *need* it. The feature that children resident in contemporary long-stay child care establishments share beyond any purported needs, however, is the fact that nearly all of them would cause considerable inconvenience to the rest of society if such provision were not available. The threshold of inconvenience beyond which children will be passed into the care of residential establishments varies according to the financial means of those inconvenienced and the cost of provision. For employers, potential disruption of parents' work may make a subsidised boarding school place cost-effective. In schools, persistent disruption and/or chronic misery may justify the cost of a boarding special school. In the criminal justice system, only persistent and/or serious offending will carry teenagers over the threshold for residence.

Thresholds are also determined by perceptions of the outcomes of residence: schools which consistently propel *alumni* into positions of wealth and authority will always have long waiting lists, whilst welfare institutions whose graduates are more likely to feature in the Court Reports than the Court Circular will have to fight harder for referrals. Demand for residential provision is thus subject to both a push and a pull: the push of the inconvenience caused to adults by children, and the pull of what the establishments can achieve for their charges. For Young Offender Institutions, push factors dominate, for eminent public schools pull factors are important. For other establishments - EBD schools, YTCs, secure community homes, ordinary community homes, psychiatric hospitals, lesser boarding schools, state boarding schools and so on - the equation is more complex.

It is in this context that Caldecott should consider its future provision. If the Community were a private company, how many investors would be rushing forth to support the enterprise? 'Only those who enjoy the thrill of high risk ventures' is the likely answer. However, a careful look at the market and at the experience of those agencies that have tried to do without residential care, such as Warwickshire, show that there is a continuing demand for residential beds for a few very difficult children. But specialisation is not, as many might expect, the natural consequence of this trend because difficult children are a heterogeneous group with different needs, as the evidence on career avenues demonstrates.

Caldecott will flourish if it diversifies further, not so much in the children it admits but in the types of services it offers local authorities and other welfare agencies. Training, expert advice, research and development will increasingly be demanded not only by residential centres trying to cope with all kinds of needy youngsters but by those offering treatment in the community. This is one possible strategy; other are now explored as the general conclusions of the study are drawn together.

Conclusions

In recent years there has been much reflection about the role of residential care for difficult and disadvantaged children and the therapeutic communities have not escaped criticism for insitutionalising children and failing to protect them from abuse. This study is one of many commissioned as policy makers and practitioners seek to re-define and improve the quality of service. As Caldecott rests partly, at least, in the special school system and follows the psychotherapeutic tradition, this study is particularly opportune because there is so little research in this area.

This research immediately raised the question of why certain children are admitted to therapeutic communities and how idiosyncratic are the referral and admission criteria. What sort of children come to be recognised as Cotswold Community, Mulberry Bush or Caldecott clients? How 'frozen' do you have to be? Unfortunately, in the past, residential care - and therapeutic communities in particular - has been more concerned with the needs to be met rather than with the needs of the child. Residential care became 'supply led' but when the supply begins to dry up, mostly for economic reasons, there is a struggle, sometimes unedifying, on the part of the residential communities to stay in business. This characterised the industrial and reformatory schools in the 1920s, the approved schools during the 1970s, the progressive and smaller independent schools during recent years and possibly the preparatory and public schools in the 1990s.

Because the clients of special provision were self-evident, because their needs were seen to be generated more from within than from without and because the system justified the provision, there was little need to evaluate outcome. It was a subtle and dangerous relationship. Normal educational and child care procedures legitimised the creation of special categories of children. We can easily forget that almost any adolescent experiences problems of adjustment, that is what makes them so fascinating. Because any scientific evaluation of a therapeutic intervention was likely to call into question both the definition of need and the underlying social processes, scrutiny of outcomes has long been avoided.

The tradition of belief in a theory rather than objective study of evidence, often coupled with a tendency to arrogance on the part of pioneers and their successors in residential care, has sealed the fate of many residential institutions. The approved schools, observation and assessment centres and some therapeutic communities deemed social work to be incapable of coping with children's difficult behaviour by means of community interventions. In spite of some cosmetic attempts to give residential care a 'new look' in recent years, disenchantment with the residential sector, among social workers and other professionals remains considerable. Dismissing external, cogent criticism as ill-informed and malevolent is counter-productive.

We have previously suggested that a renewed belief in residential care might come from clear, objective evidence of its value. There are some children whom residence cannot help; placing young offenders in children's homes or prisons has frequently been shown to have little effect and can even be damaging. But other studies at Dartington have recently shown that some children, not least extremely difficult and disturbed young people placed in the secure and specialist Youth Treatment Centres, can benefit from their stays in residence, providing certain conditions are met. Far from undermining therapeutic endeavour, asking the questions who? where? and by what process? can greatly enhance the quality of residential care and resurrect the shaken belief of those who work within its walls.

Our research approach to residential care is well-tried. We are concerned to know about the historical processes that underpin a child-care system. We take a longitudinal perspective attempting to link the backgrounds of children to their experience in residential care and subsequent outcomes. We have spent considerable time exploring and describing the types of care on offer, including the contribution of residential social workers and teachers within the Community. An enduring feature of Dartington studies has been to take seriously the child's view and the perspectives of family members. At Caldecott we were fortunate to meet such an articulate and insightful young woman as Siobhan Kelly. She has taught us much about residential care and the needs of those it shelters. Her account is the focus of this study and, hopefully, helps to unify its disparate sections.

Caldecott has a long and distinguished history and continuities abound, even over 80 years. The appointment of young and committed members of staff, the welcoming of external scrutiny, the maintenance of strong links with relatives in spite of their exclusion from life in the Community itself; all of these features, salient in the 1920s, are still apparent today. We sometimes mistakenly enthuse about the strengths of residence or complain about its weaknesses, imagining that these are recent inventions. How much easier it is to blame the deficiencies of an administrative system or a lack of resource rather than to understand the complex processes that lie beneath the surface.

Caldecott has been fortunate because its founders were far-sighted and introduced a model of care radical in its day and which still has value. In the 1940s, a visit to the Community was integral to a protection officer's training. Is it entirely beneficial that residential care plays such a small part in social work education today? The stress placed upon education, the egalitarian attitudes instilled by the Community and the search for a child's *grande passion* might still have a part in meeting the needs of troubled children.

Unfortunately, those contributing to the therapeutic tradition have seldom been at ease with each other and have frequently been at odds with those providing more orthodox care. Placed in a room together, the Freuds, Jung, Klein, Winnicott and Bowlby might have been quite as aggressive as any they sought to treat; if anything united the pioneers of special education it was their deep mistrust of each other! Not only did their approaches resist evaluation but ideas were advanced in a language which few could understand. A priority for those working in this area could be to state clearly the core values of the therapeutic tradition and the specific aims and objectives of communities within. If these efforts to spread the word are to succeed, then some element of doubt and informed scepticism should be encouraged. There is no place for arrogance. Many professionals are struggling to find answers to the problems of extremely damaged young people. The therapeutic approach is one solution, and now we have some evidence on its efficacy, but it is not the last word. If local authorities are to provide a comprehensive service for children, they need places like Caldecott; but Caldecott also needs the local authorities.

That Caldecott has engaged with the outside world is clear from its success in maintaining a place in the market place of disadvantaged children. We have seen how the Community has adapted its provision to meet the needs of several groups of youngsters over the last 80 years. The types of children obliged to rely on residential care in 1920 are now supported at home with relatives, and Caldecott beds have long been reserved for youngsters who, in a previously, would have been considered more in need of reform than care or therapy - not least victims of child sexual abuse like Siobhan. The Community adapts but strategic planning is seldom in evidence. What will Caldecott be at the turn of the century? Which children will be defined as in need of residence then?

To plan strategically, the Community will have to fully engage with the wider child-care world it serves. Caldecott shares with many residential centres a preoccupation with what goes on within its walls and shrinks from tackling the structural disadvantages of children in their home communities and from acknowledging the innovations taking place to support those in need. While nearly all other research studies are scattered with references to the *Children Act*, 1989, the most important piece of children's legislation for 20 years, it plays little part in this investigation and is insufficiently acknowledged at the Community. Volume 4 of the guidance which accompanies the Act and the change of ethos (which has pervaded even the most lack-lustre of social services departments) are still largely undiscussed at Caldecott. It may be that the Community is doing everything required but a view of the 'Act' as an irritation rather than as a sound basis for the task in hand is a dangerous and complacent attitude.

In some respects, however, Caldecott has responded to wider movements in child-care. The opening up of the Community to research scrutiny and its willingness to respond to criticism mark Caldecott apart from other residential centres and much local authority child-care provision. But more could be done, especially with regard to understanding the expectations of social services departments and others who work in the name of child protection who, after all, cope with the majority of abused children quite effectively.

Specialised residential care and wider public sector services for children are mutually dependent. Although residential care has diminished and will continue to decrease in size, there remains a small core of children who will not flourish in foster homes, with adopted parents or in less intensive forms of residential care. Whereas parents can and do choose good mainstream day schools as an alternative to residential preparatory schools, there is no obvious effective alternative for many of the children placed at Caldecott. Therapeutic communities still have a role to play but these schools will have to maintain their creativity if they are to be seen as integral to the services which a good local authority has on offer for difficult and disturbed children.

In one respect at least, Caldecott is unique. It provides a place for its graduates to return, a niche to which ex-Caldecott children can belong. Few other residential centres we know of provide children with such a sense of belonging. Indeed, we vividly remember a homeless graduate of care say he could not visit his old children's home because 'children's homes are not for the likes of me, they are for children'. Caldecott welcomes back up to 100 of its leavers every year and is still supporting some who left 40 years ago. Those local authorities struggling to comply with the *Children Act*, 1989, with the duty to assist and advise young people leaving care until their 21st birthday, could learn much from the Community's approach.

The fact that Caldecott needs to provide this support is evidence that children's problems do not go away. Those in the psycho-dynamic tradition frequently talk of 'finishing off the work'; it was a phrase we heard used in relation to Siobhan Kelly. There was a great deal more to do in the case of Siobhan but even if Caldecott had responded more fully to her disclosures and, by their reckoning, 'completed the work', the same unresolved emotions that all of us carry into adulthood would endure. When we asked Trevor Newington (who left the Community in 1960) whether or not he was happy, he hesitated. As with many adults who have been in care, we sense their feelings of loss and their constant struggle to reconcile past problems, even when on other criteria they are functioning relatively well.

Much of the burden for support after Caldecott rests with the after-care workers at the Community and ex-members of staff who formed 'special relationships' with children in their care. With the taste of scandal still fresh, residential workers hesitate to use the words 'special relationship' today but good outcomes are frequently the consequences of close bonds between staff and children. This was certainly the case for Siobhan Kelly. One man who worked at Caldecott 40 years ago said to us 'I used to put up ex-pupils in trouble. I wouldn't do that now, people would get the wrong idea'.

If ex-staff carry a burden, then those in the Community carry an enormous weight. Even a glance at those pages describing the work of residential social workers at Caldecott reveals a job which is demanding both physically and emotionally. Some might compare their situation with house-doctors in hospitals working long hours and putting up with highly stressful circumstances to learn their trade. But while house-doctors may be poor, they have prospects. Many young adults coming into residential care have far less opportunities and they have fewer choices on leaving. 'Poor with few prospects' is a label that could be applied to many residential workers today.

This is an area where there is considerable scope for experiment and improvement. The Warner report is mainly remembered for its focus on sex-offenders but its major concern was with the support offered to employees and with reviewing their progress. Clearly financial costs militate against wholesale change and residential centres in the voluntary sector could not survive if they had to match the pay and conditions offered by the public sector. Caldecott is, again, doing more than most through its innovations in the training of staff and proposals to develop the Caldecott College.

Linking with local authority residential centres is another way forward. Kent County Council has 11 special boarding schools, seven residential family support centres, eight children's homes, three adolescent units and four homes for mentally handicapped children. Surely some staff in these centres could benefit from experience at the Caldecott Community and there may be scope for those who wish to move between the two sectors. Shared training may also help. Similar co-operation with the other County Councils in the South East corner of England and some of the London boroughs might also bear fruit.

At present, we sense that staff are viewed in more of an instrumental than an expressive light. There is a contrast between the care of the children and the care of employees. Indeed, underpinning the whimsy of any therapeutic centre is a fearsome bureaucracy which helps to balance the books, achieve the right mix of children and a sufficient complement of staff. We recalled those moments when Leila Rendel had to ask staff to continue their work without pay and in the 1990s there have been constant threats of redundancy. In this context innovation and change is difficult but we are convinced that some developments in staffing can be achieved.

One way of easing the pressure on staff has been to exclude a small number of residents who become excessively violent and/or sexually precocious. This practice is most unfortunate and the pain of rejection is acute for children and is long resented by those professionals on whom Caldecott relies for referrals. Margaret Stirling sums it up when she says:

> In the course of its history the Community has found it very difficult to contain some kinds of overt violence which have put

others at risk. But if Caldecott is now a place for 'end of the road' children, where else are they to go?

In scrutinising the records it seems that some children – like Thomas Bozzi described earlier in this report – have been hastened on their way for behaviours which, if we can honestly reminisce, were among the rare and transitory compensations for the pains and boredom of troubled adolescence. Sexual issues, always the Achilles heel of residential institutions, continue to cause difficulties at Caldecott.

Residential centres shelter a *pot pourri* of children and not all of those taken under its roof can benefit. Using an approach practised in several other Dartington reports, we have identified several career avenues pursued by children at Caldecott. We have consistently found that progress in these high risk situations frequently reflects a combination of the decisions that a child (or his or her family) make and the response to these decisions by welfare and other support agencies. Such an approach incorporates both the child's pathology (the orthodox way of categorising children) and the interventions fashioned to ease his or her difficulties. The method reflects our belief that children's outcomes are to an extent predictable and that by understanding their situation at one moment in time, at least in general terms, we can say with a reasonable degree of accuracy what will be happening at a future point.

At Caldecott, children from fragmented families fare reasonably well in the long-term unless they depart before their 16th birthday to a place other than home. Victims of sexual abuse are much more prone to problems, especially those girls becoming pregnant in their teenage years. Children who come to Caldecott with behavioural difficulties have the most optimistic prognosis although, once again, those experiencing frequent breakdown and movement continue to have difficulty well into adulthood. The outlook for those long known to need protection from abuse is more mixed and these young people must navigate several avenues if they are to find long-term stability and security.

We hope that the preceding pages make a convincing case for the benefit to residential centres of using this career model. Each career requires differing inputs, not least in the emphasis given to aspects of the treatment plan, and will have differing outcomes. We hope to have identified key moments when decisions made by Caldecott, local authority personnel, the family and the child his or herself bear heavily on progress. The maps in Part Five of this book are an attempt to illustrate some of these processes.

There is much that residential social workers could do to incorporate this evidence into decision making at case conferences and other reviews and to this end we will be providing procedures to help staff identify children's career paths. Naturally, this information will form only one small part of the overall strategy for each child and will have to be combined with the treatment plan and the local authority care plan. Our hope is that staff will come to take longer-term perspectives on children and come to see the Caldecott experience as one part of the child's career rather than a make or break 'last resort'.

If the concept of career helped us trace and understand the progress of the 60 children who left the Community between 1986 and 1990, the case studies of Siobhan and others have added much detail to the picture. While much of our early thinking focused on a child's ability to disclose abuse or to gain insights into other difficulties, we have learned that several disclosures are the norm and that for every two steps forward children subsequently take at least one back. In this respect the therapeutic approach differs from that in behaviour modification settings where steady improvement clearly is the aim. At Caldecott, the picture is more uneven; the lows in this pattern form the focus of much therapeutic work for the child, for they represent periods when children are particularly vulnerable and progress can be quickly overturned.

The treatment model at the Community recognises this vulnerability. In contrast to the rather cosy picture that the term therapeutic community conjures up, Caldecott is actually a very controlling place and it employs a range of rewards and sanctions that would not be out of place in a behaviour modification system. Indeed, it is the contrast between the strict expectations of the living units and the more liberal approach found at the adolescent unit, at home or in a bedsit that frequently confounds and unnerves graduates. Further research to understand patterns of child development in long-stay residential centres would not be unwelcome, especially if it can provide practical advice on how this difficult transition for children can be eased.

Childrens' fluctuating fortunes in the Community can partly be explained by the slowly decreasing gap that exists between what children know and what they are able to tell adults. Only Siobhan knows all the details of her maltreatment; her foster mother is next best informed followed by her foster father. We know less than them, even after a long and careful study, even with access to diaries and other sensitive material. Nonetheless, Siobhan has given us a glimpse of her past life, more than she gives to most. Children carefully control and filter this information and it takes a long time before they allow outsiders access to help them understand past abuse.

The most likely source of disruption to this pattern and a child's recovery is movement, even the threat of movement. A problem which characterises almost all residential care is the propensity to transfer difficult children on the pretext that better treatment exists elsewhere in the institution. Caldecott may escape many strictures, but it cannot escape this, especially if the evidence in Part Five of this study is to be taken seriously. The Community has been characterised by an ambivalence towards and, in extreme cases, by a rejection of difficult adolescents, particularly those exhibiting sexually provocative behaviours. It also finds aggressive posturing difficult to cope with. This may be because the origins of the Community lay in work with younger children and the traditions set by a female work force. A cosy, evangelical, middle-class ethos was constructed, preoccupied with amenity and environment. Leila Rendel was concerned that her girls might spend their Sunday afternoons in the cinema or lounging in an ecstasy of moral danger in an Ashford coffee bar. Today such prissiness may raise a smile but some adolescents are still precipitately and, from our vantage point, unnecessarily moved within the Com-munity or moved from it altogether.

This problem will be a major challenge to Caldecott over the coming years; it is a challenge shared by many other residential contexts. Some units within Caldecott have discovered successful methods for coping with adolescents, especially those aged 11-14 years, primarily by adapting skills long-practised with younger children. This work needs to be developed and disseminated throughout the Community.

Finally, almost a hardy annual in Dartington's work, we stress again the importance of natural parents, wider family and home neighbourhood, resources frequently neglected by the residential sector. Much work at Caldecott has suggested that maintaining home contact has been difficult not only because of the Community's location but also because many parents were reluctant to travel and were frequently without the necessary funds and other supports for the journey. These barriers still exist.

A few children have been extremely damaged by their family experiences, meaning that re-union and even contact with certain relatives should not be attempted. These children require particular attention for their long-term progress will depend upon the variety of supports that the local authority, the Community and other substitute carers can offer. 'Residential adoption' might be a viable option for some children but if it is to succeed it should apply to a carefully selected group and come with a guarantee of the Community's determination to hang on to the child come what may. It will also need careful evaluation to compare outcomes against alternatives for this type of child.

For most children, however, the research message that most children function better, psychologically, socially and educationally, and above all are happier, if they remain in contact with their home will continue to apply. These findings are, after all, among the foundation stones on which children's legislation is now based. If we add to this our knowledge that many young people are highly likely to go back to the family at the end of their care sojourn and that those who establish themselves independently do better when they maintain links with home, the obligations on residential care to keep contacts going for the majority become overwhelming.

Moreover, family/child relationships are reciprocal and the damage and stress of separation are not only restricted to the child. It is experienced by parents, by siblings and the wider family. We have elsewhere demonstrated how difficult going home can be both for the young people and their families and unless parents retain some sense of power, responsibility and decision making while children are away, reunion will be fraught.

We would suggest that Caldecott revitalises its work in this area. There are models that can be borrowed from other settings, such as the family diagnostic sessions pioneered by the Youth Treatment Service. Most important will be a place at the Community in which families can relax, talk openly to their children and begin to engage with residential social workers about the reasons that led to placement at Caldecott becoming a necessity. Family members need to be a part of the process, to be integral to the therapeutic setting and to the work that continues once the

child has left. Better co-operation with professionals in the world outside Caldecott can also help in this respect.

For those of us who have worked long in and written extensively
about residential care, an offer to scrutinise a different context is not
always welcomed. After all, is there anything new to say? In fact, the
work at Caldecott has been extremely rewarding, not only from the new
perspectives we have gained into the children's arriving, going through
and leaving a therapeutic and special school setting but also from the
opportunity to write about these issues in an unorthodox fashion. We
hope that in some small way we have contributed to the work of
Caldecott and to its thinking about future plans. It should be encouraged by some of the findings in this report. The prospects for those arriving at Caldecott are frequently bleak and the child who died in a joy
riding accident some months after leaving the Community is a reminder
of how bad outcomes can be. Most do relatively well and some prosper.
But the transitions experienced by the children are painful as Siobhan
Kelly's story so clearly illustrates. If Caldecott can achieve as much for
other residents as it achieved for Siobhan then the future of at least this
residential centre would seem bright.

Ways forward

Not all research findings are welcome and it would be misleading for us
to claim that those associated with Caldecott viewed the results of our
exercise with unrestrained enthusiasm. Some felt that our history failed
to capture the vitality of the early days, while others felt it glossed over
the considerable weaknesses now evident in Leila Rendel's approach.
The description of Caldecott's work caused some irritation among those
with a sophisticated understanding of the psycho-analytic approach, although most workers and managers were non-committal. The career
routes were seen as helpful in differentiating between the needs of children admitted but some felt that we had overlooked other key groups.
The outcomes caused particular confusion; with nothing to gauge them
against, staff did not know whether they were good or bad. Above all
else, for all the insights we receive from Siobhan, it was frequently pointed
out that she is not typical and in any case therapeutic communities have

not always been dazzlingly successful at protecting vulnerable children. In addition, we heard the oft expressed criticism of research findings that they were true when the study was undertaken, but they are not true now.

Nonetheless, Caldecott has decided to act on the findings of this study. It is also encouraging that continuing investigations will, in future, inform developments at the Community. It is recognised that, if Caldecott is to continue to be a catalyst for services for vulnerable children in the United Kingdom, it will have to reconsider its role and change provision in at least four areas. These closing messages may be relevant to others who seek to provide an innovative residential service.

First, the Community is seeking to diversify, to include in its provision other much needed services such as training, research and consultancy. The opening of the Caldecott College to enhance the professional development of Community staff will also act as a centre of learning for others in the residential sector. The incorporation of research, by the recruitment of Ph.D. students and by becoming the first large residential centre in England routinely to use the Department of Health's *Looking After Children* monitoring and review materials, is another.

In time, it is envisaged that a teaching hospital model will develop, thus bringing about the second fundamental change in the Caldecott service. The aim is to bring onto one campus children, families, residential workers, consultants, teachers and researchers and, by effective communication, to break down the barriers and overcome the misunderstandings that currently exist. To this end, Caldecott is reviewing the suitability of its accommodation in the mansion house.

In line with the findings of this study, Caldecott is to re-think its relationship with others in the child-care field and to set about a process of integration with the various groups seeking to support troubled children and families. Integration with local authority services, with other therapeutic communities and specialist centres and with those who seek to find new ways of supporting children in need, not least those responsible for legislation and guidance, is now recognised as essential to the Community's well-being.

Finally, Caldecott has recognised the value of identifying the various groups of children it shelters and of clearly setting out manageable aims and objectives for each individual. For a small minority who should not return to relatives, this will mean finding ways of supporting children well into adulthood. For the majority for whom contact with relatives is beneficial, improvements in the quality of family work are being introduced and a place within the Community for parents to visit, stay and participate in the treatment programme is being developed in one of the new purpose built units on the campus.

It is expected that these developments will take place and that they will lead to better outcomes for youngsters placed at the Caldecott Community and an improved understanding of the needs of troubled children. It may be impossible for Caldecott graduates to find 'a life without problems' but, this study has shown that the Community's continued commitment to children and to new methods of support and treatment can achieve some progress in this difficult area of work.

Epilogue

"

Myself

Full name	Siobhan Emma Kelly
Date of birth	18.4.78
DOD	24.7.93
Eyes	Blue
Hair	Blonde, shoulder length
Height	5.2 ft.
Weight	8½ stone (roughly)
Family	Four older brothers, mum and dad divorced
Music	Not modern music, more into 60's etc.
Food	Houmous, corn on the cob
Place	Bedroom
Friends	Pascale, Hayley, Abigail, Shirley, Louise Jenna, Sharon
Books	Books on dreams and horoscopes
TV prog	Home and Away, Neighbours, Casualty, The Bill etc. etc.
Sport	Any – volleyball, badminton, basketball
Hobbies	Aerobics, sleeping, listening to music.

References

Anderson, E and Morgan, A (1987) *Provision for Children in Need of Boarding/Residential Education*. Boarding Schools Association

Balbernie, R (1966) *Residential Work with Children*. Human Context Books

Baldwin, N (1990) *The Power to Care in Children's Homes*. Avebury

Barker, P (1974) *The Residential Psychiatric Treatment of Children*. Crosby Lockwood Staples

Beedell, C (1970) *Residential Life with Children*. Routledge and Kegan Paul

Beedell, C (1993) *Poor Starts, Lost Opportunities, Hopeful Outcomes*. The Charterhouse Group

Berridge, D (1985) *Children's Homes*. Basil Blackwell

Berry, J (1975) *Daily Experience in Residential Life*. Routledge and Kegan Paul

Bettleheim, B (1950) *Love is Not Enough: The Treatment of Emotionally Disturbed Children*. Free Press

Bowman, I 'Maladjustment: a history of the category' in Swann, W ed. (1981) *The Practice of Special Education*. Basil Blackwell

Bridgeland, M (1971) *Pioneer Work with Maladjusted Children: a Study of the Development of Therapeutic Education*. Staples Press

Broad, B (1994) *Leaving Care in the 1990s: the Results of a National Survey*. Royal Philanthropic Society/ Aftercare Consortium

Buckholdt, D and Gubrium, J (1979) *Caretakers: Treating Emotionally Disturbed Children*. Sage

Bullock, R, Hosie, K, Little, M and Millham, S (1990) 'The problems of managing the family contacts of children in residential care', *British Journal of Social Work*, 591-610

Bullock, R, Little, M and Millham, S (1993) *Going Home: The Return of Children Separated from their Families*. Dartmouth

Bullock, R, Little, M and Millham, S (1993) *Residential Care for Children: a Review of the Research*. HMSO

Carlebach, J (1970) *Caring for Troubled Children*. Routledge and Kegan Paul

Cawson, P (1978) *Community Homes: A Study of Residential Staff*. HMSO

Cliffe, D with Berridge, D (1991) *Closing Children's Homes: an End to Residential Child Care?* National Children's Bureau

Cole, T (1986) *Residential Special Education*. Open University Press

Colton, M (1988) *Dimensions of Substitute Child Care*. Avebury

Cooper, P (1993) *Effective Schools for Disaffected Students*. Routledge

Davenport Hill, F (1868) *Children of the State; the Training of Juvenile Paupers*. Macmillan.

Department of Health and Social Security (1971) *Care and Treatment in a Planned Environment*. HMSO

Department of Health (1991) *Children in Public Care* (The Utting Report). HMSO

Department of Health (1991) *The Children Act Guidance and Regulations. Vol 4. Residential Care*. HMSO

Department of Health (1992) *Choosing with Care. Report of the Committee of Inquiry into the Selection, Development and Management of Staff in Children's Homes* (Warner Report). HMSO

Dockar-Drysdale, B (1968) *Papers on Residential Work: Therapy in Child-Care*. Longman

Dockar-Drysdale, B (1990) *The Provision of Primary Experience: Winnicottian Work with Children and Adolescents*. Free Association Books

Gottesman, M (1991) *Residential Care: An International Reader*. Whiting and Birch

Grimshaw, R with Berridge, D (1994) *Educating Disruptive Children : Placement and Progress in Residential Schools for Pupils with Emotional and Behavioural Difficulties*. National Children's Bureau.

Her Majesty's Inspectors of Schools (1989) *A Survey of Provision for Pupils with Emotional/ Behavioural Difficulties in Maintained Special Schools and Units.* Department of Education and Science

Her Majesty's Inspectors of Schools/ Audit Commission (1992) *Getting in on the Act. Provision for Pupils with Special Educational Needs: the national picture.* HMSO

HMSO (1946) *Report of the Care of Children Committee* (Curtis Report). HMSO

Hoghughi, M (1988) *Treating Problem Children.* Sage

Kahan, B (1979) *Growing up in Care.* Blackwell

Kahan, B (1994) *Growing up in Groups.* HMSO

Kashti, Y and Arieli, M (1976) *Residential Settings: Socialization in Powerful Environments.* Daga

King, J (1993) 'A father to the fatherless' *Therapeutic Care and Education*, 2 ,1 , 270–281

King, R, Raynes, N and Tizard, J (1971) *Patterns of Residential Care.* Routledge and Kegan Paul

Lambert, R and Millham, S (1968) *The Hothouse Society.* Weidenfeld and Nicolson

Levy, A and Kahan, B (1991) *The Pindown Experience and the Protection of Children.* (Report of the Staffordshire Child Care Inquiry 1990). Staffordshire County Council

Local Government Management Board (1992) *The Quality of Care* (Howe Report). Local Government Management Board

Main, T (1975) 'Some psychodynamics of large groups' in Kreeger, L ed. *The Large Group.* Constable

Main, T (1977) 'The concept of the therapeutic community: variations and vicissitudes', *Group Analysis*, vol. X, no. 2

Manning, N (1989) *The Therapeutic Community Movement: Charisma and Routinisation.* Routledge

Menzies, I (1960) 'A case study in the functioning of social systems as a defense against anxiety', *Human Relations*, 13:95-121

Menzies, I (1970) *The Functioning of Social Systems as a Defence Against Anxiety.* Tavistock Institute of Human Relations

Millham, S, Bullock, R and Cherrett, P (1979) *After Grace - Teeth. A Comparative Study of the Residential Experience of Boys in Approved Schools.* Human Context Books

Miller, D (1994) *Attack on the Self: Adolescent Behavioral Disturbances and their Treatment.* Jason Aronson

Millham, S, Bullock, R, and Hosie, K (1980) *Learning to Care: the Training of Staff for Residential Social Work with Young People.* Gower

Millham, S, Bullock, R, Hosie, K and Haak, M (1981) *Issues of Control in Residential Child-Care.* HMSO

Millham, S, Bullock, R, Hosie, K and Haak, M (1986) *Lost in Care.* Gower

Monsky, S (1963) *Staffing of Local Authority Residential Homes for Children.* Central Office of Information

Moss, P (1975) 'Residential care of children: A general view' in Tizard, J, Sinclair I and Clarke, R eds. *Varieties of Residential Experience.* Routledge and Kegan Paul

National Institute for Social Work (1988) *Residential Care: A Positive Choice* (Wagner Report: Vol. 1). HMSO

Parker, R (1988) 'Children' in Sinclair, I ed. *Residential Care. The Research Reviewed* (Wagner Report Vol 2). HMSO

Parker, R (1990) *Away from Home: A History of Child-Care.* Barnardos

Parker, R, Ward, H, Jackson, S et al. *eds* (1991) *Looking after children: Assessing Outcomes in Child Care.* HMSO

Pinchbeck, I and Hewitt, M (1969) *Children in English Society* (2 volumes). Routledge and Kegan Paul

Petrie, I (1962) 'Residential treatment of maladjusted children', *British Journal of Educational Psychology*, 32, 27-39

Quinton, D and Rutter, M (1988) *Parenting Breakdown*. Avebury

Rose, M (1990) *Healing Hurt Minds: the Peper Harow Experience*. Tavistock/Routledge

Rutter, M (1975) *Helping Troubled Children*. Penguin

Rutter, M, Tizard, J and Whitmore, K *eds* (1970) *Education, Health and Behaviour*. Longman

Rutter, M, Taylor, E and Hersov, L (1994) *Child and Adolescent Psychiatry: Modern Approaches* (3rd edition). Blackwell

Stirling, M (1991) 'Absent with leave', *Special Children*, November, 10-13

Thoburn, J (1991) 'Survey findings and conclusions' in Fratter, J, Rowe, J, Sapsford D and Thoburn, J *Permanent Family Placement*. BAAF

Westcott, H (1991) *Institutional Abuse of Children ; from Research to Policy*. NSPCC

Whitaker, D, Cook, J, Dunn, C and Lunn-Rockliffe, S (1984) *The Experience of Residential Care from the Perspective of Children, Parents and Care-givers*. University of York

Whittaker, J (1979) *Caring for Troubled Children: Residential Treatment in the Community*. Jossey-Bass

Williams Committee (1967) *Caring for People: Staffing Residential Homes*. Allen and Unwin

Wills, D (1971) *Spare the Child*. Penguin

Index

Isaacs, S., 34

Jinks, M., 25, 38, 39, 119
Jung, C., 202

Kelly, Siobhan
   background of, 5, 10, 12-14; career route of, 82, 167-8; diary
   of, 5, 7-8, 13-14, 57-59, 66-71, 87-97, 131-140, 151-3, 183-5,
   189-193; discloses abuse, 87-98; family of, 7, 8, 13-4, 57-9, 68,
   88, 90, 91, 95-6, 108, 133, 135, 138, 140, 154-5, 184, 193;
   peer group, 68-71; referral, arrival and departure at Caldecott,
   57-9, 66-8, 153-5
Kelmer Pringle, M., 34, 36
Kent County Council, 35, 73, 205
King, J., 21, 25-6, 36-8, 119, 126, 157
Kitty, 92, 111, 122
Klein, M., 99
Knatchbull family, 41

Lacton Hall, 11, 39, 42, 60, 61, 144, 145, 147, 148, 151, 180, 182,
   192
Lacton House, 11, 42, 181
Lake View, 1
Leila Rendell Fund, 26, 27, 183
Leopold Muller House, 42
Levy, A., and Kahan, B., 119, 126
Lloyd, E., 17, 18, 20, 26
London Jewish Hospital, 47
London School Board, 17
Looking After Children, 211
Long-term protection cases, 82, 108, 171-2, 174
Lyward, G., 49

Maggs, P., 39, 133
Main, T., 106
Martin, D., 23
Maudesley Hospital, 34, 62

Mayfield, 60, 61, 92
Mersham-le-Hatch, 18, 21, 41, 42, 43, 47, 98, 141-2
Monsky, S., 122
Moss, P., 194, 196, 197
Mote, The 19, 41
Mulberry Bush, The 100, 200

Newington, T., 27-31, 117, 155, 204
Nuffield Educational Trust, 35

Oaklea, 1

Paddington Clinic, 34
Parker, R., 17, 48, 194
Pavlov, A., 102
Peper Harow, 100, 101
Pinchbeck, I., 17
Pindown Report, 72
Potter, P., 17-20, 24-6
Priestley, J.B., 33
Psycho-analytic theory of behaviour, 99-100
Psychotherapy, 10, 79, 100-1, 192

Rendel, L., 9, 10, 17-26, 32-8, 40, 47, 49, 50-1, 53-4, 71, 75, 99,
        123, 147, 205, 208, 210
Richmond, Tina, 69, 88-9, 97, 137, 142, 143, 180
Rodway, S., 20, 25-6, 30
Rowson, R., 20
Rutter, M., 36

Siobhan, see Kelly
Skinner, B.F., 102
Social Learning Theory, 103
Stagg, G., 51
Stirling, M., 17, 19, 20-1, 24-5, 37-8, 206
Stokes, Sir W. 22
Summerhill, 24